Discovering
THE
GOLDEN
COMPASS

BOOKS BY GEORGE BEAHM

The Vaughn Bode Index (Heresy Press, 1975)

Kirk's Works: The Art of Tim Kirk (Heresy Press, 1977)

How to Sell Woodstoves (George Beahm, 1980)

How to Buy a Woodstove—and Not Get Burned (George Beahm, 1980)

Notes from Elam (GB Publishing, 1983)

The Great Taste of Virginia Seafood (GB Publishing, 1984)

Write to the Top: How to Complain and Get Results—Fast!
(Donning, 1988)

The Stephen King Companion (Andrews McMeel, 1989)

The Stephen King Story (Andrews McMeel, 1991)

The Stephen King Story: A Literary Profile
(updated and revised, Andrews McMeel, 1992)

Michael Jordan: A Shooting Star
(Andrews McMeel, 1994)

The Stephen King Companion
(revised & expanded, Andrews
McMeel, 1995)

Books by George Beahm

The Unauthorized Anne Rice Companion
(Andrews McMeel, 1996)

Stephen King: America's Best-Loved Boogeyman
(Andrews McMeel, 1998)

Stephen King from A to Z (Andrews McMeel, 1998)

Stephen King Country (Running Press, 1999)

Stephen King Collectibles (Betts Books, 2000)

The Unofficial Patricia Cornwell Companion (St. Martin's Press, 2002)

*Straight Talk about Terrorism: Protecting Your Home and Family from Nuclear,
Biological, and Chemical Attacks* (Potomac Books, 2003)

The Essential J. R. R. Tolkien Sourcebook (New Page Books, 2004)

*Muggles and Magic: An Unofficial Guide
to J. K. Rowling and the Harry Potter Phenomenon* (Hampton Roads, 2004)

Fact, Fiction, and Folklore in Harry Potter's World: An Unofficial Guide
(Hampton Roads, 2005)

Passport to Narnia: A Newcomer's Guide (Hampton Roads, 2005)

The Whimsic Alley Book of Spells (with Stanley Goldin, Hampton Roads, 2007)

Muggles and Magic: An Unofficial Guide
(3rd ed., significantly revised and expanded, Hampton Roads, 2007)

Caribbean Pirates: A Treasure Chest of Fact, Fiction, and Folklore
(Hampton Roads, 2007)

Stephen King Collectibles
(2nd ed., revised and expanded, Betts Books, 2007)

Stephen King: American Storyteller
(Flights of Imagination, 2007)

Quiet Courage: My Mother's Story
(forthcoming, 2008)

STORIES ARE THE MOST IMPORTANT THING IN
THE WORLD. WITHOUT STORIES, WE WOULDN'T
BE HUMAN BEINGS AT ALL.

—Philip Pullman

Discovering
THE
GOLDEN
COMPASS

A Guide to
Philip Pullman's
Dark Materials

George Beahm
art by Tim Kirk

HAMPTON ROADS
PUBLISHING COMPANY, INC.

This book is not endorsed, approved, or authorized
by New Line Cinema, Scholastic Books, Random House,
or any of it subsidiaries, partners, or licensees.
Tim Kirk inside cover and interior art © 2007 by Tim Kirk
"I have a feeling all of this belongs to me" by Philip Pullman
originally appeared in the *Something about the Author* autobiography
series from Thomas Gale. Reprinted by permission
of AP Watt, Ltd., on behalf of Philip Pullman.
All photos of Oxford, credited or uncredited, are © 2007 by Emma Raynaud
Photographs by Tiffany Vincent © 2007 by Tiffany Vincent
All other uncredited photos © 2007 by George Beahm
Transcript of Oxford Talk by Nicola Priest © 2007 by Nicola Priest

Cover design by Steve Amarillo
Cover art by Tim Kirk

Hampton Roads Publishing Company, Inc.
1125 Stoney Ridge Road
Charlottesville, VA 22902

434-296-2772
fax: 434-296-5096
e-mail: hrpc@hrpub.com
www.hrpub.com

If you are unable to order this book from your local
bookseller, you may order directly from the publisher.
Call 1-800-766-8009, toll-free.

Library of Congress Cataloging-in-Publication Data

Beahm, George W.
    Discovering The golden compass : a guide to Philip Pullman's Dark materials /
George Beahm.
        p. cm.
    Summary: "Many people are newcomers to Philip Pullman's world of His Dark
Materials. In Discovering the Golden Compass, readers will easily chart their way into
a parallel universe and explore the streets of another Oxford with Lyra, Roger, and the
Gyptians; see their own daemons; make friends with armored bears; and glimpse
unworldly cities through the Northern Lights"--Provided by publisher.
    Includes bibliographical references and index.
    ISBN-13: 978-1-57174-506-4 (acid-free paper)
    1. Pullman, Philip, 1946- His dark materials--Handbooks, manuals, etc. I. Title.
PR6066.U44Z54 2007
823'.914--dc22
                            200702069

ISBN 978-1-57174-506-4
10 9 8 7 6 5 4 3 2 1
Printed on acid-free paper in Canada

TO MARY AND LINDA

CONTENTS

PART 4: DÆMON DRIVEN: ENCOMPASSING PHILIP PULLMAN

PART 5: POINTING THE WAY TO *THE GOLDEN COMPASS* ON THE SILVER SCREEN

PART 6: POINTING THE WAY TO THE MANY WORLDS OF HIS DARK MATERIALS: MULTIPLE PRESENTATIONS

PART 7: POINTING THE WAY TO TRUE NORTH: RESOURCES

APPENDICES

Emma Raynaud

A Note to Newcomers

ANYONE TRYING TO NAVIGATE HIS WAY THROUGH
THE FILM ADAPTATIONS OF HIS DARK MATERIALS—
WITHOUT HAVING READ THE BOOKS—IS GOING TO
NEED HIS *OWN* GOLDEN COMPASS.

—Jennifer Vineyard, for MTV.com

ennifer is right.

This book is your own golden compass to His Dark Materials, comprised of three books: *The Golden Compass* (399 pages), *The Subtle Knife* (326 pages), and *The Amber Spyglass* (518 pages), totaling 1,243 pages (based on the U.S. trade editions). Since 1995, these books have sold fourteen million copies and won numerous prestigious awards.

If you are planning to see *The Golden Compass* at the movie theater or planning to read the trilogy and want to know more about Pullman and his fiction, be forewarned that there are dozens of books already out on His Dark Materials, most of them written for scholars, with subjects and approaches catering to the academic community.

There's even a 542-page encyclopedia, *The Elements of His Dark Materials,* by Laurie Frost, a necessarily detailed and definitive book that explores every nook and cranny of the trilogy. Due to the complex, ambitious, and thought-provoking storyline of His Dark Materials, it doesn't lend itself to simplified explanations or abbreviated plot summaries. Although Frost's book is an outstanding resource, it's not for the casual reader. (For the hardcore fan, though, it's simply indispensable.)

I think what the average newcomer to the Pullman universe wants to know is a little about the books and the author, so as not to feel totally lost and disoriented, like Alice who fell down a rabbit hole and found herself in Wonderland.

I hope you'll be interested enough in Pullman's ambitious and magnificent story to want to explore further and find out more about the storyteller and His Dark Materials, which is why I've written this book—your passport to Pullman's imaginative universe.

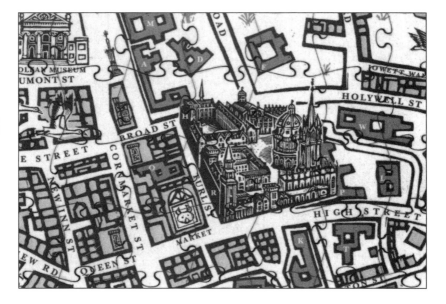

*A closeup of Jordan College in a wooden puzzle
made by Longstaff Workshops*

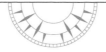

EXPANDED CHRONOLOGY

NOTE: All book dates refer to U.K. editions, unless specifically stated otherwise.

1946 Phillip Pullman is born in Norwich, England, on October 19, the first son of Alfred Outram Pullman and Audrey Evelyn Merrifield.

1948 Phillip's brother Francis is born.

1952 The Pullman family moves to Southern Rhodesia (now Zimbabwe) when his father, a pilot for the Royal Air Force, is transferred.

1954 Flight Lieutenant Alfred Pullman, age thirty-eight, is killed in combat in operations against the Mau Mau in Kenya.

The Pullmans move back to England; at a ceremony in Buckingham Palace, Queen Elizabeth II presents Mrs. Pullman, on behalf of her late husband, the Distinguished Flying Cross.

The Pullmans move into a London apartment. Mrs. Pullman finds full-time work in London, and her two boys go to live with their grandparents, the Reverend Sidney Merrifield, an Anglican clergyman, and his wife. Pullman fondly remembers Rev. Merrifield as a wonderful storyteller and "the most importance influence in my life." Rev. Merrifield exposed the boys to the Bible, the *Book of Common Prayer,* church, and Sunday School.

1955 Mrs. Audrey Pullman remarries another RAF pilot, whose orders send him overseas. The Pullmans travel by ocean liner to Australia, where Philip is exposed to popular culture: radio dramas and American comics (notably Superman, Batman, and Captain America). Philip is struck by the melding of the comic book format—a marriage of words and pictures, like a movie storyboard, that he realizes is a dramatic way to tell stories—and becomes hooked on comics. The Pullman family grows by three, with the addition of a brother, sister, and stepbrother.

1957 After Mrs. Pullman's husband retires and returns to England, they move to Llanbedr in northern Wales. Philip attends a prep school in Battersea, followed by Ysgol Ardudwy, a state school in Harlech, Gwynedd.

After acquiring a copy of *The History of Art,* Philip begins drawing in earnest, discovering his latent talent as an artist. His English teacher, Enid Jones, exposes Philip to poetry, notably *Paradise Lost.* Philip is enraptured by its imagery and narrative power.

1965 Philip begins his first year at Exeter College (Oxford University). He hopes to get an education in writing but is disappointed with the curriculum and wishes he had pursued studying art instead. (He would go on to become a self-taught artist.)

1968 Philip graduates from Exeter with a bachelor of arts degree. He optimistically begins a novel that, unrealistically, he feels will bring him instant fame and riches. He discovers that reading fiction and writing it are worlds apart; the writing quality of his first novel is poor and he subsequently abandons it. He is forced to seek full-time employment to make a living and secures a job in London at Moss Brothers, renting and selling formal men's clothing. He meets the future Mrs. Pullman at a party.

1970 Philip marries the former Judith Speller on August 15. A teacher, she encourages him to get his teaching certification, which he subsequently does at the Weymouth College of Education.

1971 The Pullmans' first son, James, is born.

1972 Philip publishes his first novel, *The Haunted Storm* (New English Library), which is a joint winner of the New English Library's Young Writer's Award. A judge, Lady Antonia Fraser, called it a "serious book" and "refreshingly free of triviality." She concluded that Philip Pullman "seems to me, therefore, to have the real makings of a writer."

Fraser's early praise notwithstanding, Philip Pullman has since repudiated the novel, which is permanently out of print. In fact, he refuses to mention its title in interviews and prefers it remain buried in the past.

1974 Pullman obtains his teaching certification from Weymouth College of Education and begins teaching middle school (children aged nine to thirteen). He wrote and produced school plays, including *Count Karlstein, The Firework-Maker's Daughter,* and *Spring-Heeled Jack*—all of which would be subsequently published in book form.

1978 Philip publishes his second adult novel, *Galatea* (Gollancz).

1979 Philip (with co-editor and illustrator Ivan Ripley) publishes *Using "The Oxford Junior Dictionary": A Book of Exercises and Games* (Oxford University Press).

1981 The Pullmans' second son, Thomas, is born. Philip publishes *Ancient Civilizations* (Wheaton), illustrated by Gary Long.

1982 Philip publishes *Count Karlstein* (Chatto and Windus).

1984 Pullman's play *Sherlock Holmes and the Adventure of the Sumatran Devil* is produced at Polka's Children's Theatre in Wimbledon.

1985 Pullman's play *Three Musketeers* (from the Dumas novel) is produced at Polka's Children's Theatre. Philip edits Detective Stories (Kingfisher Books) and publishes *The Ruby in the Smoke* (Oxford University Press), the first of four Sally Lockhart novels, which he describes on his website as "old-fashioned Victorian blood-and-thunder."

1986 Philip publishes the second Sally Lockhart novel, *The Shadow in the Plate* (Oxford University Press), which is republished in 1988 as *The Shadow in the North.*

1987 Philip publishes *How to Be Cool* (Heinemann), and he produces *Frankenstein* at Polka's Children's Theatre.

1988 Philip begins part-time work as a lecturer at Westminster College (a job he holds through 1996).

1989 Philip publishes *Spring-Heeled Jack* (Doubleday). He pitches David Fickling on the idea of an ambitious trilogy and receives a sizable book advance.

1990 Philip publishes a play adaptation, *Frankenstein* (Oxford University Press), and *The Broken Bridge* (Macmillan Children's Books).

1991 Philip publishes the third Sally Lockhart novel, *The Tiger in the Well* (Viking Children's Books).

1992 Philip publishes a play adaptation, *Sherlock Holmes and the Limehouse Horror* (Nelson), *The White Mercedes* (Pan Macmillan), and a reissue of *Using the "New Oxford School Dictionary."*

1993 Philip publishes *The Wonderful Story of Aladdin and the Enchanted Lamp* (Scholastic), with illustrations by David Wyatt.

1994 Philip publishes the fourth (and last) Sally Lockhart novel, *The Tin Princess* (Puffin).

1995 Philip publishes *The Firework Maker's Daughter* (Doubleday); the first New Cut Gang novel, *The Gas-Fitter's Ball* (Viking), illustrated by Mark Thomas; and *Northern Lights,* the first of three books that comprise His Dark Materials.

1996 Philip publishes *Clockwork* (Doubleday), illustrated by Peter Bailey. In the U.S., *The Golden Compass* (Knopf) is published (its original title in the U.K. was *Northern Lights*). Its success allows Philip to write full-time. (He had previously taught part-time as a senior lecturer in English at Westminster College at Oxford University.)

1997 Philip publishes *The Subtle Knife,* the second novel comprising His Dark Materials.

1998 Philip publishes *Mossycoat* (Scholastic Hippo), illustrated by Peter Bailey, and *The Butterfly Tattoo* (Macmillan Children's Books).

1999 Philip publishes *I Was a Rat! . . . or The Scarlet Slippers* (Knopf), illustrated by Peter Bailey.

2000 Philip publishes *Puss in Boots* (Doubleday), illustrated by Ian Beck, and the third book comprising His Dark Materials, *The Amber Spyglass* (Scholastic).

2003 Philip publishes *Lyra's Oxford* (Scholastic), which he describes on his website as "a sort of stepping-stone between the trilogy [His Dark Materials] and the book that's coming next [*The Book of Dust*]. *Lyra's Oxford* is "beautifully illustrated" (as he noted on his website) with wood engravings by John Lawrence.

2004 Philip publishes *The Scarecrow and His Servant* (Doubleday).
    In the New Year Honors List, he is made a Commander of the British Empire (CBE).

The National Theatre opens its most ambitious production, an adaptation of His Dark Materials, which is highly successful.

The Pullmans, seeking much-needed privacy, leave Oxford and move to nearby Cumnor, where they buy an old farmhouse.

2005 Philip wins the Astrid Lindgren Memorial Award, shared with Japanese illustrator Ryoji Arai.

2007 Philip receives the Honorary Freedom of the City from Oxford City Council. In March, Philip speaks at the Oxford Literary Festival, where he's joined by *The Golden Compass* film producer Deborah Forte to talk about the challenges in adapting his book to the movie screen.

December 7, New Line Cinema releases *The Golden Compass* as a major motion picture.

2009 Projected publication date, according to Philip Pullman, of *The Book of Dust.*

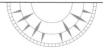

Dark Matter, Dæmons, and Dust: The Many Worlds of Philip Pullman

Artist rendering of the Stardust satellite pursuing a comet

 t's called Stardust and, after traveling 2.9 billion miles, the space capsule returned to Earth carrying its precious cargo dating back "4.6 billion years to the dawn of the solar system" (*Popular Mechanics*, Nov. 2006). These interstellar dust samples were obtained by using a very fine screen to capture the dust from a comet halfway to Jupiter. The dust is dark material and it's at the core of Philip Pullman's imaginative, mind-stretching books published as His Dark Materials.

The cover to the U.S. edition of The Golden Compass, *with art by Eric Rohmann*

I first encountered *The Golden Compass* at a Barnes & Noble bookstore on Merchant's Square in Williamsburg, Virginia, in 1995.[1]

A large stack of handsomely jacketed copies of *The Golden Compass* commanded my attention. Eric Rohmann's compelling art showed a polar bear with preternatural intelligence, on his back a young girl, bundled against the cold, with a companion mouse. What, I thought, would a mouse be doing on the back of a polar bear? Is there such a thing as an arctic mouse? (Actually, there is. It's the Svalbard field mouse, *Microtus epiroticus.*)

The book's liner notes breathlessly announced that "Pullman's *The Golden Compass* is a masterwork of fantasy and storytelling that heralds the arrival of a classic." The back cover featured endorsements, including one by fantasy author Terry Brooks who presciently wrote, "I foresee much success for the series and its talented author." Similarly, Newbery Medalist Lois Lowry was clearly smitten with the book's "endearingly spunky heroine and her charming variable sidekick, who made me long for a personal dæmon myself."

What, I wondered, is a dæmon? And why would Ms. Lowry *want* one?

The hardback book cost $20, which was more than I wanted to pay at that time, as my book budget for that month had already been grossly exceeded. So I reluctantly passed; ten years later, I bought that first edition copy—for $85 on eBay.

What I couldn't know back then was that His Dark Materials would go on to win prestigious awards both in the United States and United

---

[1] Interestingly, that same year, a young woman in England wrote a short fantasy novel about a boy attending a wizarding school called Hogwarts and sent it out to prospective publishers and agents, all of whom rejected it.

Kingdom; and that with each passing year, its popularity would rise unabated until its cumulative sales would exceed fourteen million in print, a figure that will skyrocket after *The Golden Compass* is released as a movie.

What I also didn't know at that time was that Pullman bristles at the notion that he's written a fantasy novel. Yes, there are fantasy elements, but the intent of the book, he steadfastly maintains, is "stark realism." (It's an important and necessary distinction to keep in mind.)

Pullman's objections aside, it became clear that he had accomplished something rare and celebratory: writing a book with fantastic elements that appealed to both children and adults, without pandering to either group. *The Golden Compass* raised the expectations of readers; they would no longer be happy with the tried and true literary fare, the traditional and (let's be honest) significantly less imaginative cousins. Moreover, Pullman had raised the writing bar considerably: no one writing fantastic fiction could simply write another imitation of *The Lord of the Rings* and be taken seriously. As the *Boston Globe's* William Flesch pointed out, in "Childish Things" (June 13, 2004), "The mystery isn't why so many adult readers are reading these books, but rather why more adult writers aren't writing anything nearly as ambitious."

It's not really much of a mystery. Writing a story as challenging as His Dark Materials would tax even the most seasoned writer. Pullman himself didn't tackle the project until he was in his late forties, by which time his life experience, his skill at storytelling, and his fiction-writing skills came together beautifully.

—⟫◆⟪—

Pullman took an innovative approach to His Dark Materials. He chose to write a work with fantastic elements that took its inspiration principally from John Milton's *Paradise Lost,* an epic poem that "undertakes to encompass the whole of mankind—war, love, religion, Hell, Heaven, the cosmos" *(The Norton Anthology of English Literature).*

His Dark Materials reflects similar themes and cosmography, and therein lies its great appeal: not only to children whose minds are challenged and nourished by such imaginative fare, but also to adults who can appreciate it on multiple levels. In *Talking Books,* Pullman himself termed His Dark Materials as *"Paradise Lost* for teenagers."

Make no mistake: His Dark Materials may have been initially packaged and marketed as a children's book, but it's nothing of the sort. It is, in fact, an important work of fiction in its own right, and should not be confused with standard fantasy fare. That, I believe, explains why so many people have responded with enthusiasm to His Dark Materials. It also explains Philip Pullman's serious intent as a novelist who plays down the association of the book to children's literature and clearly wishes to disassociate himself from the fantasy field in general. "I don't like the 'fantasy' label," he wrote in a letter to me, and added, "I've said before that His Dark Materials is a work of realism, not fantasy, and it has nothing whatever in common with Tolkien or any of his imitators."

In fact, the only notable similarity between Tolkien's epic fantasy *The Lord of the Rings* and Pullman's His Dark Materials is that both are single stories published as trilogies. The books are otherwise worlds apart: Tolkien's linguistically inspired book is an engaging, straightforward epic quest, whereas Pullman's classically inspired book is a complicated, multilayered cosmic quest. Therefore it stands to reason that Tolkien would have numerous imitators, whereas Pullman will likely have none: Tolkien is far easier to imitate.

If there was any doubt that Pullman had raised the stakes with *The Golden Compass,* the publication of *The Subtle Knife* and *The Amber Spyglass* put that doubt forever to rest. Moreover, the books finally allowed Pullman, then fifty years old and teaching part time, to devote all his time and attention to writing. Because His Dark Materials was considerably different from what he had published before, Pullman imagined it would have a small readership, but he was wrong. The critical and financial success of His Dark Materials fundamentally changed Pullman's life, bringing him to the attention of a worldwide audience that clearly hungered for substantial literary fare, a grand and ambitious story that dealt with the essence of human existence: birth, life, death, and the afterlife.

The public now clamored for more. Besieged by reporters, by fans, and by publishers who wanted him to blurb their books and write introductions, Pullman discovered that fame has its downside. After a lifetime of relative anonymity, he was suddenly thrust into the limelight and became a figure of great curiosity and interest. He is now a worldwide celebrity.

The cumulative result of such attention, which is flattering up to a point, is that a writer stops being a servant to the story and becomes a servant trying to fill too many public demands on his most precious commodity—time.

In an August 2005 posting on his website, Pullman finally acknowledged the problem, the burden of ever-increasing time distractions that kept piling up when Pullman couldn't, or wouldn't, say no. Among them: writing a new introduction to the Oxford University Press edition of *Paradise Lost*; attending the Dorchester Festival at which he would answer questions; giving a lecture at the Centre for the Children's Book; attending a book fair in Sweden; and giving a lecture to the Blake Society in London.

Finally, Pullman realized that, although all of these things are worthwhile, it took precious time away from his main priority: telling stories. He had to make a draconian decision, or his own writing output would suffer drastically. As Pullman explained in August 2005 in his e-newsletter to readers of his website:

> Now that all adds up to too much, frankly, and I shouldn't have agreed to any of it. But once all these things are over, NO MORE. FINISH. DONE.
>
> Because to my regret I keep on making the same discovery: that I cannot write AND give lectures and so on. One, yes. Both, no. And I'm going to make *The Book of Dust* my absolute priority from October on. It is now, almost, apart from just these few remaining things. Very soon, the drawbridge will come up, the phone will be disconnected, the shutters will close.

And that is as it should be: Leave the writer alone to tell the tales, spin the stories. The work should *always* come first. And if it doesn't, then the writer has unwisely strayed off his chosen path.

———◈———

Pullman is currently holed up in his new home outside Oxford and, with the exception of an appearance in May 2007 at the annual Oxford Literary Festival, he's hard at work on *The Book of Dust*. When published, it will be embraced by legions of Pullman fans who, in the interim, have had their appetites whetted by a small but handsome book, *Lyra's Oxford*.

On December 7, 2007, the ranks of Pullman's fans will swell by millions more when New Line Cinema releases its film adaptation of *The Golden Compass*. It stars Nicole Kidman as Mrs. Coulter, Daniel Craig as Lord Asriel, and a newcomer, Dakota Blue Richards, in the pivotal role of Lyra.

As Pullman tells us, there are many more stories he has to tell in exploring his fictional universe of His Dark Materials, where there are dæmons and dust, armored polar bears, curious creatures of every kind, bewitching witches, a host of heavenly (and not so heavenly) angels, and unspeakable evil.

This book is your introduction to Pullman's universe in all its beauty and wonder and terror. Immerse yourself in His Dark Materials comprised, and in search of, the very stuff of life—stardust.

George Beahm
Williamsburg, Virginia
May 22, 2007

An angel, a graphic used for a cube manufactured
for the National Theatre production of His Dark Materials

PART 1

POINTING THE WAY TO PHILIP PULLMAN AND HIS DARK MATERIALS

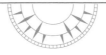

PHILIP PULLMAN:
SERVANT OF THE STORY

I'M IN THE "ONCE UPON A TIME" BUSINESS.
—from the official Philip Pullman website

 NCE UPON A TIME . . .

. . . AN AMBITIOUS YOUNG MAN NAMED PHILIP PULLMAN, ATTENDING OXFORD, DECIDED HE WOULD WRITE A NOVEL, WITH THE EXPECTATION THAT "IT WAS GOING TO BE PUBLISHED BEFORE THE END OF THE YEAR, AND THE FILM RIGHTS WOULD BE SOLD FOR A MILLION POUNDS, AND I'D BE FAMOUS AND RICH, JUST LIKE THAT. IT WAS A GOOD PLAN."

But as English poet Robert Burns observed, the best-laid schemes of mice and men often go astray. The ambitious novel was never completed and, like other aspiring writers, Pullman was forced to fall back on an alternate plan. "I grudgingly admitted the need to earn a living, and that was when my real education began."

Like many other writers, Pullman found work at a mundane job; in his case, working at Moss Brothers in London, a store that sold men's formal wear. But during his lunch breaks and in the evening, he'd write, and this time he did so with a more realistic assessment of what it took to write well—never mind becoming famous. Disciplining himself to write three pages a day (approximately a thousand words), Pullman wrote, and subsequently published in 1972, his first novel, *The Haunted Storm*. Long out of print, a secondhand copy can fetch up to $4,000 on the antiquarian market, depending on its condition. But by Pullman's choice, the book will forever remain out of print, despite offers from publishers to reissue it. An adult novel, *The Haunted Storm* was a joint winner of New English Library's Young Writer Award, which raises the question: *Why* does Pullman think so poorly of it?

Philip Pullman's second book, Galatea

In 1978, Pullman published a second adult novel, *Galatea*. Among its advocates was the *Glasgow Herald,* with these words of praise: "The first thing to hook me was the quality of the writing. Philip Pullman has written a fantasy, a quest, with a particularly lucid prose. No small achievement."

The book would be Pullman's last contemporary work for more than ten years. From 1982 to 1995, Pullman's varied output included nonfiction books for children *(Ancient Civilizations* and *Using "The Oxford Junior Dictionary"),* fairy tales, children's books, historical thrillers (the Sally Lockhart novels and the New Cut Gang), and plays. These early books sold respectably but not spectacularly, with the result that writing was his avocation. A teacher for twelve years and a lecturer in a college of education for six, Pullman wrote in the evenings and on weekends, building up an impressive list of books to his name, but their cumulative sales did not allow him to realize his dream: to write full time.

Pullman's life changed when he pitched the idea of a long, ambitious novel to Scholastic's David Fickling, who enthusiastically backed it with a hefty advance for the three books.

Inspired by a single image, Pullman then began writing in his studio, a modest garden shed behind his house. As he told Steve Meacham ("The shed where God died") in the *Sydney Morning Herald*, "I began with the idea of a little girl hiding somewhere she shouldn't be, overhearing something she shouldn't hear. I didn't know then who she was, where she was, or what she overheard. I just started writing. Before too long I realised I was telling a story which would serve as a vehicle for exploring things which I had been thinking about over the years. Lyra came to me at the right stage in my life."

In 1995, Pullman published *Northern Lights,* which was immediately hailed as a literary tour de force that, finally, shook off the long mantle of J. R. R. Tolkien, whose trilogy has heavily (some say excessively) influenced the field of epic fantasy since 1954. *Northern Lights* would go on to win both the Carnegie Medal and the Guardian Award for children's fiction.

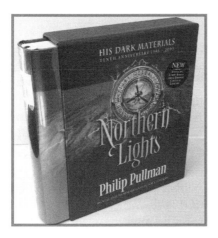

The signed, limited edition of Northern Lights, *published in the U.K.*

5

A year later, *Northern Lights* would be published in the United States under a new title, *The Golden Compass.*

The cover to the U.S. edition of The Golden Compass, *with art by Eric Rohmann*

Newbury Medalist Lloyd Alexander, quoted on the back jacket of the Knopf hardback edition of *The Golden Compass,* wrote: "I'm enormously impressed. It's a rich combination of high fantasy, high drama, and intense emotion. Philip Pullman's creation is a world thoroughly realized, completely convincing. Best yet, this volume promises to be the beginning of an ongoing major literary effort. Readers can only wait impatiently."

Deliberately marketed as a children's novel, *The Golden Compass* incorporated a story line with a cosmic concern: the nature of life. Despite its otherworldly elements and imaginary trappings, *The Golden Compass,* Pullman insisted, is fantastical but it's *not* fantasy fare, and therefore shouldn't be confused with books so labeled. As Pullman explained to Steve Meacham of the *Sydney Morning Herald,* "Despite the armoured bears and the angels, I don't think I'm writing fantasy. I think I'm writing realism. My books are psychologically real. So I would be most flattered if I was compared to George Eliot, Jane Austen, or Henry James. But I don't expect anybody will."

The problem, of course, was that the critics, not to mention the children, saw things quite differently: If there are witches, cliff-ghasts, talking bears, dæmons, and otherworldly inventions like alethiometers, how can it *not* be fantasy?

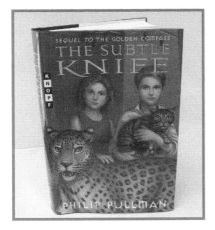

The cover to the U.S. edition of **The Subtle Knife,** *with art by Eric Rohmann*

In 1997, when *The Subtle Knife* was published, the story line had necessarily become increasingly complex, building on what had gone before. Lyra, her dæmon Pantalaimon, and their new companion, Will, explore parallel universes through the device of the subtle knife, a one-of-a-kind blade of extraordinary power with a unique capability—it can cut windows into other worlds.

The cover to the U.S. edition of **The Amber Spyglass,** *with art by Eric Rohmann*

In 2000, the final book, *The Amber Spyglass,* was published. The longest and most ambitious of the three, *The Amber Spyglass* dealt with religious and metaphysical ideas, and the nature of Dust: at stake, the fate of Lyra's world, and millions of other worlds as well. A literary tour de force, *The Amber Spyglass* won both the prestigious Whitbread award for best children's novel and Book of the Year—an unprecedented event.

Delighting and amazing readers of all ages, outraging Christians who

7

viewed Pullman and His Dark Materials as heretical, and mystifying critics who couldn't figure out the category in which the books should be placed (children's books or adult books, fantasy or realism?) or how to take Pullman's adamant assertion that His Dark Materials should be taken seriously as realistic fiction, Pullman and His Dark Materials forever changed the face of children's book publishing.

Taken as a whole, His Dark Materials exposed readers to a fully realized world that, upon closer inspection, has a lot more in common with our own than not. "War, politics, magic, science, individual lives, and cosmic destinies are all here . . . shaped and assembled into a narrative of tremendous pace by a man with a generous, precise intelligence. I am completely enchanted," wrote Margo Jefferson in the *New York Times Book Review.* Millions of other readers worldwide were similarly enchanted.

To understand His Dark Materials, one must first understand the writer, his life, and his formative influences. And who better to tell us about Pullman than Pullman himself?

T-shirt designed for the stage production of
His Dark Materials, *produced by the National Theatre*

I HAVE A FEELING THIS
ALL BELONGS TO ME

by Philip Pullman

Emma Raynaud

bout three years before I began to write the first part of His Dark Materials, an American reference book publisher asked me to write an autobiographical sketch. It was the first time I'd thought about my life in that sort of way, and I guessed that (with a bit of luck) I was roughly halfway through that life; so it seemed like a good time to stop and take stock of where I'd come from and how I'd got to where I was.

So here it is. What I didn't know then, of course, was what was going to happen when His Dark Materials was published. Everything changed after that. But this is a true account of the preparation for writing that story.

One day when I was a little boy I went out for a walk with my grandmother. There was a big pile of dark brown earthenware pipes by the side of the road for the workmen to put underground, and Granny let me clamber about over them for a while and crawl inside and out the other end. But she was anxious to go back home, and I couldn't persuade her to stay, so I went with her, reluctantly; and when we got home, who could believe it? I had a new brother. A little crying baby, of all things. Where had he come from?

My mother was hanging out some washing on a sunny day, and singing, as happy as a lark. The wind was chasing fat white clouds

9

through the blue sky, and the sheets on the line billowed like the clouds, big fresh-smelling moist clouds that swelled and flapped and swung up high. The song my mother was singing filled the sheets and the clouds and the immense blue beaming sky, and I felt so light that I too might swing up and be blown along in the wild blue splendour; and she took me and swung me up, high up among the snowy-white sheets and the billowing clouds and the wind and the song and the endless dazzling sky, and I shouted and sang for joy.

Forty years later, when I was writing a book called *The Broken Bridge,* I wanted to give my character Ginny an image of perfect happiness; and nothing I'd experienced in all my life was better than the sheets and the clouds and the song and the bright blue morning, so I wrote about them in the same words that I've used here.

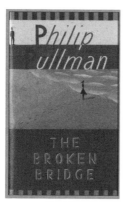

The cover to The Broken Bridge (Dell Laurel-Leaf)

There was a girl who took me down to the tall grass at the end of her garden and kissed me. I thought that meant we had to get married, but later, not yet; and I was conscious that that made me more grown-up than I was, and I felt both pleased and resigned at the same time. Oh, is everything decided already, then?

I always liked girls. At one point I wanted to be a girl myself, and I even picked a name: I was going to be Margot. But from the laughter that greeted this announcement I got the idea that wanting to be a girl was strange and embarrassing, and that there were some things I'd better keep to myself.

I didn't know what girls were like until another little girl showed me. I was about to show her what I was like when her mother came along and found us. The moment she appeared I knew what we were doing was terribly wrong, yet a moment earlier I had had no idea of that, not the slightest notion.

———⊱◈⊰———

My father was in the Royal Air Force, and when I was six he was posted to Southern Rhodesia, which is now Zimbabwe. My mother and brother and I went too, and I found myself going to a school where we had to wear little trilby hats as part of the uniform. That wasn't strange, because everyone else had to. But there was a ghost in the school, and that was strange. One day a boy had gone to the headmaster's study and opened the door when he shouldn't have done, and the headmaster had slammed the door on his wrist, cutting off his hand. The boy had died, of course, and now he had haunted the corridor ever since.

There was another ghost in a little electrical substation at the edge of town. It was a locked concrete building that emitted a constant electrical hum. An African had gone in there despite the red lightning bolt warning sign on the door and had been electrocuted. So that place was haunted too, and the electrical hum has been ghostly for me ever since.

Africa was full of strange things. There was a little theatre where my mother acted in drawing-room plays put on by the amateur dramatic society; I saw her there one morning, crying bitterly while a strange man shouted at her, and I didn't know how to help her or what to do at all, and then someone explained that it was only a rehearsal, she was only acting, and everything was all right.

———⊱◈⊰———

Sometimes my father would take us to the compound, where the Africans lived, to see a boxing match. There was a ring of ropes in which two men with big gloves stood hitting each other. We would pick one to cheer for. In the evening the most beautiful smell in the world, roasting mealies (corn on the cob), would drift out from the compound into the place where the white people lived. I loved that smell so much that when years and years later I happened to smell it unexpectedly in a street market in London, where someone was roasting mealies to sell, I found tears springing to my eyes.

The smell of mealies was kindly and nourishing, but it didn't intoxicate like the smell of glamour. There were two kinds of glamour: my mother's, which consisted of a scent called Blue Grass by Elizabeth Arden, and my father's, which was more complicated. There were cigarettes in it, and beer, and leather armchairs. The smell of my father's glamour was very strong in the Club, which we children were sometimes allowed in, but not to run around.

I wanted to smoke like the grown-ups, so my father bought me a packet of ten cigarettes. I suppose he hoped I'd get so sick I'd never want another one, but I smoked them all one after the other and loved them. He wouldn't give me any more, but he did let me sip his beer. I liked that too.

In the Club they had little dishes of peanuts you could help yourself to, and some other nuts called cashew nuts, which I thought were a more glamourous kind of peanut. Another thing we used to eat was biltong, which is a kind of sun-dried meat, or beef jerky. It looks like strips of dark leather. You can't imagine how delicious it is.

But one thing they didn't have in Africa was fried bread. Granny used to make fried bread, and I missed it, and I was glad to go home to England when my father's tour of duty ended if only to taste fried bread again. Granny and Grandpa lived in Norfolk. Grandpa was the rector of a village called Drayton, and they lived in a grand house called the Rectory with Granny's sister, who was simply known as Auntie. Every Sunday my brother and I would walk with Granny to church for the eleven o'clock matins while Auntie cooked the Sunday lunch, and Auntie would go on her own to the six o'clock evensong.

Auntie had a weak heart. She told us it had been broken when she was a young lady. I never found out if that was true, but it explained why it was weak. Once a year she went to a convent for a week to stay with her friends, the nuns, and that was her holiday. She never married. I offered to marry her myself, because I loved her a lot, but she gently turned me down.

One thing that both Granny and Auntie did was to change their clothes in midafternoon. At about half-past three they'd go upstairs and have a rest and come down later in different dresses. That seemed to me such an elegant thing to do that it was very nearly glamourous.

Both Granny and Auntie, and my brother and I, and everyone else for that matter, regarded Grandpa as the centre of the world. There was no one stronger than he was, or wiser, or kinder. People were always calling to see him, for a parish priest was an important man, after all. He led the church services in his cassock and white surplice; he took weddings and funerals and christenings; and he was the chaplain of Norwich Prison (though I didn't find out about the prison until much later, when I was old enough). When I was young he was the sun at the centre of my life.

He told stories. . . .

He took the simplest little event and made a story out of it. When he was a young man in Devonshire before the First World War he'd had a friend called Fred Austin, a fine horseman, a big strong man with a fierce moustache, and he and Grandpa had joined the army together to fight in France. When Fred came home to his farm after the end of the war, the baby he'd left behind was now a little girl who didn't know him and was frightened by this big dark laughing man who knelt and held out his enormous hands for her. She ran away and hid her face, but Fred was a wise man and didn't hurry. Little by little over the next days he coaxed her and was kind and gentle, and finally she came to him trustfully. When Grandpa told that story he said that God would appear to us like that; at first we'd be alarmed and frightened by him, but eventually we'd come to trust in his love.

Well, many years later, when Grandpa and Fred Austin were both long dead, I used to tell the story of the *Iliad* to the children I taught; and there's a part of that story where the great Prince Hector goes up on the walls of Troy to watch the battle below and finds his little son Astyanax in the arms of his nurse. He reaches for the boy, but Astyanax is frightened by the great nodding plumes on his father's battle helmet and hides his face in the nurse's shoulder until Hector, laughing, takes off the helmet and reassures the little child. Whenever I told that story, I used to think of Grandpa's story about Fred Austin. Between my childhood and now, I've lost sight of God; but Hector the Trojan prince and Fred Austin the Devonshire soldier are still brightly alive to me, and so is Grandpa.

One sunny morning my brother and I were playing on the wall of the rectory garden when Auntie called us inside. My mother was crying, and Granny explained that it was because a telegram had come from Africa saying that my father had been killed. I understood that his plane had been shot down, because I knew this was a time when the British were fighting in Kenya against a political movement called the Mau Mau. I suppose that my brother and I cried, though I didn't really feel sad. The fact was that we hadn't seen my father for a long time, and apart from the glamour surrounding him, he was a figure who hadn't played much part in our lives. So my brother and I went back out to the sunny wall, where we'd been picking off the moss and throwing it at each other, and carried on.

13

And so began the next part of my life. My brother and I were to live in Norfolk with Granny and Grandpa and Auntie, while my mother went to London to get a job. She worked at the BBC and lived in a flat in Chelsea, and once or twice we went to stay with her and saw another dimension of glamour. She had lots of friends, and they were all young and pretty or handsome; the women wore hats and gloves to go to work, their dresses were long and flowery, and the men drove sports cars and smoked pipes, and there was always laughter, and the sun shone every day. Into the middle of this there came an invitation from the Queen. My father had been posthumously awarded a medal called the Distinguished Flying Cross, and the Queen was going to present it to my mother, and my brother and I were invited to attend the ceremony at Buckingham Palace.

My brother and I wore little grey suits with short trousers, and my mother wore a very glamourous black dress, because she was a widow. We arrived at Buckingham Palace by taxi, and a tall man in a uniform told us what we should do: We must bow when the Queen came into the room, and he showed us how to do that and watched as we practised; we must shake her hand, and if she spoke to us we must speak politely back and call her Ma'am, pronounced "Mam"; and we must bow when she left.

We understood that this was a special occasion, because our father had been so heroic and important. Normally the Queen gave out medals in a big public investiture, and we were allowed to stay and watch while she did that afterwards; but ours was a private investiture, which was a great honour.

So the Queen came in and shook our hands and spoke to our mother and gave her a medal in a little blue case. We bowed and shook her hand just as we'd been told, and when we came out of Buckingham Palace there were photographers from all the papers, and we posed holding the medal.

One curious thing about growing up is that you don't only move forward in time; you move backwards as well, as pieces of your parents' and grandparents' lives come to you. And it was only when I was a grown man that I found out more of the truth about my father, and I don't suppose I shall ever know the whole of it. Apparently he had been in all kinds of trouble: He'd borrowed money without being able to repay it, his affairs with other women were beginning to get out of his control, and he had had to agree to a separation from my mother. I knew none of this while my mother was alive; I've found it all out in the past few years since she died. So all my life I've had the idea that my father was a hero cut down in his prime, a warrior, a man of shining glamour, and none of it was true. Sometimes I think he's really still alive somewhere, in hiding, with a different name. I'd love to meet him.

But when I was nine years old there came a new man whom we had to learn to call Daddy. We had known him in Africa as Uncle Johnny, and he was an airman too, a friend of our father's. But we didn't know him well, and we were unsure about this new relationship for a long time, though he was kind and we tried to be polite. Having another father meant that we had to leave Granny and Grandpa and Auntie, because there was more traveling to come. As my father had been posted abroad by the Royal Air Force, so was my stepfather; and we were off to Australia.

I was too young to remember much of our first sea voyages to and from Africa, but I remember a lot about the voyage to Australia. This was in the 1950s, when it was still more common to travel by sea than by air, and how grateful I am to have lived at a time when, if you made a long journey, you traveled on the surface of the earth. One thing we've lost with air travel is a sense of how large the world is, and how various. Five miles up in a jumbo jet, what can you see? The in-flight movie, that's what you can see. But aboard ship the world was close, and all our senses knew it.

Taste, for example. When you woke up, the cabin steward brought you a cup of tea and two biscuits, and then you washed and dressed and went to breakfast, where you had a different menu every day, with lots of different kinds of bread alone: fried bread almost as good as Granny's, but also soda bread, and croissants, and brioches, and wholemeal rolls, and milk bread, and rye bread, and Hovis, and toast and . . . then at midmorning the stewards would bring around ice cream or beef tea, according to whether it was hot or cold. Then there was lunch, which was even bigger than breakfast. Then there was afternoon tea, which you had in the forward lounge. There were trolleys of cakes and pastries and little triangular sandwiches, eaten daintily while you listened to a piano trio playing selections from the musicals. Then there was dinner, which was even bigger than lunch. The grown-ups who stayed up late to dance or play bridge had even more to eat, because at 10:00 p.m. the stewards laid out plates of sandwiches in the lounges and the bars; and if you simply had to eat anything in between, there were little dishes of peanuts (both plain and glamourous) like those I remembered from the Club in Africa.

And the men in white shirts and black bow ties, the women in coloured dresses with bare shoulders, the music of the dance band, the smells of cocktails and cigarettes and Blue Grass.

But nothing was more exciting than making a landfall. After days of steadily beating through the sea, the ship would alter its motion; the ever-present creak would quieten; even the light would change; there'd be a different smell in the wind: trees, vegetation, swamp. We would all crowd to the rail and watch the line of land come closer and turn into a mountain, a city, a port . . . a foreign land! With foreign faces on the quayside, and a strange language in the air, and advertisements for unheard-of drinks and cigarettes on the hoardings. They even rowed their boats around the harbours differently—short choppy strokes in this place, long graceful sweeps in another. We would go ashore and spend strange money on souvenirs of sewn leather or carved wood, or ride in a taxi with open windows through which boys threw flowers as they ran along beside us.

We went through the Suez Canal. Camels, palm trees, Arabs in robes. We stopped at Port Said, and the gully-gully men came aboard. They were conjurers who did magic with live chicks. They performed on the deck in the hot night air, and the lights of the port glittered nearby.

⇒◇⇐

Then there was the ocean. So many different colours! So many different kinds of waves! And the different ways they made the ship move. Rolling from side to side was all right; you got used to that. But when the bow rose high and then plunged down sickeningly only to groan and rise again towards the next inevitable plunge, you stopped thinking of food and glamour and wanted to die. Then there were days and nights when the sea was as flat as a map, when the sun glared and the stars blazed.

It was on one of those calm days that we Crossed the Line (the equator). This was an important occasion. King Neptune himself came aboard, with his mermaids and sea horses, and set up his court beside the swimming pool. Passengers who hadn't Crossed the Line before had to be ducked in the pool, and if they were men they had to be shaved as well with a bucket of foam and a huge wooden razor. My brother and I had Crossed the Line before, but we were allowed to take part in the fun all the same. After the ceremony you were given a certificate promising you the help and protection of King Neptune and all the kippers and haddocks and other finny denizens of the deep.

I have too many memories of my time at sea to include them all here, but I'll add two more. One is of a sailor who showed me how to sweep a floor. I was watching him sweep up some dust, and I wanted to try, so he lent me his broom and told me that you always sweep the dust away from you, never towards you. I've done that every time I've swept a floor since. The other memory is of a girl my age. She was called Geraldine. She was dark-haired and pretty, and the first day we were aboard the ship I saw her and fell in love. And partway through the voyage, somewhere in the Indian Ocean, one of the other children showed us all how to play Postman's Knock, and so the very thing I most desperately wanted came about: I was able to kiss Geraldine. I must have been eight years old. And I vividly remember thinking as I kissed her in that half-darkened cabin how lucky I was, that I had only to think of a thing and it would happen; and that sense of being blessed by fortune has never entirely left me.

In Australia I made a great discovery. TV hadn't yet reached Australia, but everyone listened to the radio, and the drama serials used to keep us enthralled. There was "Clancy of the Outback"; there was "Dick Barton"; but the best of all was "The Adventures of Superman." "Faster than a speeding bullet! More powerful than a locomotive! Able to leap tall buildings in a single bound! Look! Up there in the sky! Is it a bird? Is it a plane? No—it's SUPERMAN!" When one day my stepfather bought me a Superman comic, it changed my life. I'd been a reader for a long time, but a reader of books; I'd never known comics. When I got this one, I devoured it and demanded more. I adored them. I adored Superman, and Superboy, and Captain America, and Dick Tracy, but most of all I adored Batman. Those poorly printed stories on their cheap yellowing newsprint intoxicated me, enthralled me, made me dizzy with passion.

What did I love? I ask myself now. Did I want to *be* Batman? Did I want to be Robin? (Surely not.) Did I want to live in that strange futuristic metropolis, Gotham City, where freakish villainy jostled on the sidewalks with sensational glamour?

No. What I wanted was to *brood* over the world of Batman and dream actively. It was the first stirring of the storytelling impulse. I couldn't have put it like this, but what I wanted was to take characters, a setting, words, and pictures and weave a pattern out of them; not *be* Batman, but write about him.

I didn't know that gruesome and wonderful fairy tale "The Juniper Tree" then, but I would have recognised one thing in it. The father is eating the stew that, unknown to him, contains the flesh of his son, and he says: "Oh, this stew is delicious! You shan't have any of it. I have a feeling this all belongs to me!" I knew that feeling. I knew instinctively, at once, that the telling of stories was delicious, and it all belonged to me.

I shared a bedroom with my brother then, and every night when the lights went out I used to tell him a story that I made up as I went along. I don't know whether he enjoyed it, or whether he even listened, but it wasn't for his benefit; it was for mine. I remember vividly the sense of diving into the dark as I began the story, with no idea at all what was going to happen or whether the story would "come out" as I called it, by which I meant make sense or come to a neat end. I remember the exhilaration of the risk: Would I find something to say? Would I dry up? And I remember the thrill, the bliss, when, a minute ahead of getting there, I saw a twist I could give to the end, a clever way of bringing back that character who'd come into it earlier and vanished inconclusively, a neat phrase to tie it all up with.

Many other things happened in Australia, but my discovery of storytelling was by far the most important.

———⟫◆⟪———

When after a year or two we moved back to England, we lived for a short time in London and then made another move, to a village called Llanbedr on the coast of North Wales, where we were to stay for ten years: the longest time I'd ever spent in one place.

Having moved around so much, I was used to leaving friends and finding my feet in a new school, or so I thought. But on my first day at Ysgol Ardudwy, I got into a fight because of my English accent.

"Where d'you come from?" said an older boy.

"London," I said, and the next thing I knew we were fighting. Apparently they didn't approve of Londoners.

Later on I became friends with that boy, and indeed with most of the other boys I had fights with. I don't think it was a violent school, but there did seem to be a lot of fights in the playground. At one time

I became anxious about it, and it was Grandpa who came to my aid. He'd been a boxer in his youth, and he showed me how to guard my jaw and jab and punch effectively, and from that time on, I knew I could defend myself. I'm sure he was right to do this. Fighting isn't the right response to bullying—for adults. Adults have to find out what makes the bully the way he is and look for reasons and answers and understanding. That's an adult's responsibility. But children who are being bullied have enough to cope with; we shouldn't expect them to shoulder the burden of understanding and sympathising with the bully's rotten home life at the same time that they are being beaten up. What children need most is the feeling that if they're attacked they can at least prevent themselves from being too badly hurt, and if the way to do that is to hurt the bully, so be it. However, I'm writing of a time when bullies used their fists. What you do to stop a bully with a knife or gun I don't know, and I don't think Grandpa would have known either. That's a different world.

The Ashmolean Museum, the oldest museum in Britain

My friends and I seemed to be free in those days to wander where we liked: the woods, the wide hills, the miles of beach were open to us, and the edge of our playground was the horizon. We roamed the hills and broke into a derelict house where the last occupant had left a Welsh Bible and a set of false teeth on the kitchen table. We made go-carts, or trucks as we called them, and hauled them up slopes (there were plenty of those) and hurtled down recklessly. We dared each other to walk past the Hanging Tree in the clearing in the woods at night. We swam in the sea; we swam in the river; we invented a new sport, waterfall climbing. We put pennies on the railway line and retrieved them, flat and distorted and shiny, after the train had gone over them. We hung about the bus shelters in the local town on Saturday night, spying on the lovers. We went to the tiny cinema in the next village and came back on the last bus, running down to the bus stop clutching bags of chips from the fish-and-chip shop, losing our footing, skidding along on the gravel with the chips held triumphantly to our chests. We held spitting contests out the window of the school train. We held grass-bomb fights at night: a handful of grass and a careful tug, and you had a very satis-factory clump of earth to hurl through the air at the dimly seen enemy across the field. We teased the short-tempered pig in the farmyard by the river. We put fireworks on the roof of the ladies' toilets. We howled like banshees in the garden of cross old Mr. Pugh till he came out and chased us away.

One winter afternoon when I was eleven years old, I saw a dead man. We lived in the woods about a mile and a half from the village, and I was walking home from school on my own when a motorcyclist went past me and five minutes later came back again and stopped.

"There's a dead man on the road up there," he said. "I'm going to phone for help. I'm just warning you."

And he rode away. I had a choice at that point in the road, for there was a path that led a different way home, and I thought of going that way instead, because the darkness was gathering. But I thought I might never have a chance like this again. A real dead body! So I walked up the road and looked at him as he lay quite peacefully on the grass verge. I suppose he'd had a heart attack.

It was around that time that our family began to get bigger, as a new brother and sister were born; and then my stepfather's son from his first marriage came to live with us, too, so I had one brother, one half-brother, one half-sister, and one stepbrother. At the time I didn't see this, but my parents must have managed things pretty well, because we all got on without any resentments or jealousies, and for that matter, we still do. It helps that we're all so different.

But of all the things I remember from those years, the most excit-ing came when I discovered art.

The visual arts, first. I was fifteen when I became interested in the history of painting. I got a book token for Christmas and exchanged it for a book called *A History of Art,* and that book (which I still have—battered and falling to pieces) became more precious to me than any Bible. It was all I had to go by, because Llanbedr is a very long way from museums and art galleries, and I pored over the little black-and-white illustrations and the few colour plates so intensely that I wonder I didn't scorch the pages. And I drew obsessively, the landscape, mainly: the massive rounded hills, the wide pearly estuary, the tumbled sand dunes, the dry stone walls, the ancient church half-buried in the sand. I learned that landscape by drawing it, and I came to care for it with a lover's devotion. Later in *The Broken Bridge* I wrote about a girl making the same discoveries, loving and drawing the same landscape. Many other strands went into the making of that book, but what lay at its heart was love; it's a love letter to a landscape.

Then there was poetry. Some of it came to me through Miss Enid Jones, who taught English at Ysgol Ardudwy. I owe her a great debt. Reading Milton and Wordsworth and the metaphysical poets under her guidance took me to places I had never dreamed of, places even richer and more glamourous than Port Said, Colombo, and Bombay. I'm thinking especially of Milton when I remember lines such as:

High on a Throne of Royal State, which far

Outshone the Wealth of Ormus and of Ind,

Or where the gorgeous East with richest hand

Showrs on her Kings Barbaric Pearl and Gold,

Satan exalted sat.

I can recall the same physical thrill I felt then. And it is physical: my skin bristles; my hair stirs; my heart beats faster. I feel my body moving to the rhythm. When I first became aware that language could do that, that words had weight and colour and taste and shape as well as meaning, I began to play with them, like a little child putting coloured marbles into patterns. I had no patience with free verse: I wanted the most ornate and complex verse forms, the most demanding rhyme schemes. I wrote sonnets and rondeaus and villanelles; I wrote heroic couplets and blank verse and ballades and sestinas. I learned enormous amounts of poetry by heart; I developed a great respect for craftsmanship.

For a long time I thought I was a poet, but that's a high title to claim. What I do say is that I can write verse, and that the writing of verse in strict form is the best possible training for writing good prose. Why? Because writing verse teaches you to recognise rhythms and cadences, which are just as important in prose, but much harder to get right. For that reason you can't write with music playing, and anyone who says he can is either writing badly, or not listening to the music, or lying. You need to hear what you're writing, and for that you need silence.

———⊱◆⊰———

When the time came to apply for university, I was in no doubt about what I wanted to study: it was English, of course. And I was in no doubt that I wanted to go to Oxford. No one in my family had ever been to university before, never mind Oxford or Cambridge, but I wanted to go, and that was that. I had to take a scholarship examination and then go for an interview, and I remember the bright winter's day, the pale sun on the old stone buildings, the air of casual and slightly shabby grandeur. When I heard just before Christmas that I'd been awarded a scholarship, I was monstrously pleased with myself.

Now I know that I made a mistake. The tutorial system that they had at Oxford required you to see your tutor once a week for an hour and read aloud an essay on some subject that you'd been set the week before: that's all. No lectures, no seminars, no classes of any other kind. (They existed, of course, but you didn't have to go to them, and it wasn't easy to find out where they were held, either. Nor did I ever find out how to use the library.) My tutor was an affable man, but he didn't like telling me that my essays were hopeless, so the only time he commented on my work was when, by accident, I wrote something good. I wasn't subtle enough to understand that: I thought it meant I was doing well. But it wasn't long before I found out that I didn't enjoy English as much as I'd thought I would, anyway. I was doing it because I wanted to learn how to write, but that wasn't what they were interested in teaching.

What I should have done, I realise now, was go to art school and learn to paint and to draw. But the way to that had been barred years earlier at school. Art was for those who weren't clever. If you were clever, you had to do Latin. I don't regret the Latin, but I do regret missing the art.

So I didn't enjoy my English course, and I didn't get a good degree, but it wasn't entirely a waste of time. I got drunk; I played the guitar; I made some good friends, some of whom are still speaking to me. And it was at Oxford that I decided that my real goal was not writing poetry but storytelling. I had a plan in mind: I was going to begin a novel on the morning after the last of my final examinations and finish it a month or so later. It was going to be published before the end of the year, and the film rights would be sold for a million pounds, and I'd be famous and rich, just like that. It was a good plan.

So I bought a big book to write in: three hundred pages of beautiful smooth lined paper in a stout binding, like a family Bible; and I sat down on the first morning of my life-after-education and began to write. And before I'd got to the end of the first paragraph, I'd come up slap bang against a fundamental problem that still troubles me today whenever I begin a story, and it's this: where am I telling it *from?*

Imagine the storytelling voice as being like a camera. A film director has to decide where to put the camera and what it's going to look at, and it's the same with the storytelling voice. How close do you want to get to your characters? Are you going to move your consciousness into this man's head and tell the readers what he's thinking? And if you can do that with one person (which is a very strange thing, if you think about it: nothing like that happens in "real life"), are you going to do it with someone else? Where are you going to stop? How do you decide where to start?

I was like the centipede who was asked which foot he put down first. I couldn't move. There were so many possibilities, and nothing to tell me which was the right one. What a shock! I had passed through the entire British education system studying literature, culminating in three years of reading English at Oxford, and they'd never told me about something as basic as the importance of point of view in fiction! Well, no doubt it was my fault that I got a poor degree; but I do think someone might have pointed it out. Perhaps it had been covered in one of those lectures I hadn't found my way to.

What I couldn't help noticing was that I learned more about the novel in a morning by trying to write a page of one than I'd learned in seven years or so of trying to write criticism. From that moment on, my respect for novelists, even the humblest, has been considerably greater than my respect for critics, even the most distinguished.

But it all meant a setback to my grand plan, of course. I grudgingly admitted the need to earn a living, and that was when my real education began.

I moved to London and worked for over a year in a large shop that sold and rented expensive men's clothes and formal dress. My job consisted of taking an order form from a pneumatic tube and hurrying around the stacks and rails of clothes to find the right sizes and colours—black tailcoat forty-four long, striped trousers thirty-six by thirty-two—then snatching a shirt and collar from the shelf, tucking a black or grey tie in the top pocket, and hanging them on the rail and chasing off for the next. The stacks were immense long structures made of scaffolding poles three racks deep. To get to the top you had to climb through swaying lines of dinner jackets and trousers and tailcoats and morning coats. You could hide in there. At a pinch you could live in there.

You certainly wouldn't have wanted for food, because the shop was in Covent Garden right next to the old central fruit and vegetable market, and the shop staff took advantage of it. One old man who was theoretically employed in the packing department never packed a thing but spent all his time smuggling watermelons, pineapples, and every other kind of fruit into the shop and selling it cheaply to the rest of us.

My fellow workers were the most mixed group of people I've ever known. As well as the Pineapple King, there were unemployed actors, who'd work there for six weeks or so before getting a small part on TV or in a provincial theatre; there were several Mauritians (including an ex-police sergeant with a beautiful tenor voice) whose language gave me the oddest sensation that it was transparent, because I could understand it—until I realised that they were speaking French. And there were a lot of gay men, including four or five Australians, small men with brightly coloured clothes and loud cries like tropical birds. I had never come into contact with a confident homosexual culture before, and I found it enchanting: yet another kind of glamour. And there were travelers: drifters from around the world working in London for a spell before moving on to America or Turkey.

One of these was a New Zealander called Nick Messenger. He and I got talking one day in the staff canteen, and we've been talking ever since. Now we talk by letter, because he's back in New Zealand. He's a poet and a painter, and when we met he'd just arrived from walking around South America and had a sheaf of poems in hand—exuberant, powerful, oceanic writing that I admired immensely.

And I was writing too. Every lunch hour, I'd go and sit in the churchyard opposite the shop and write a rondeau, just to keep my hand in. In the evening I'd write my novel. I discovered a method that's worked for me ever since: to write three pages every day, no more, no less. If you can't think of what to write, tough luck; write anyway. If you can think of lots more when you've finished the three pages, don't write it; it'll be that much easier to get going next day.

And in one way my life hasn't changed since then. I still write three pages every day, and I suppose I will till the day I die.

But I didn't want to stay in the shop forever, fun though it was. I got a job in a library for a while, where everything was quieter and more respectable and I had to wear a tie. By that time I had married Jude, and we'd had a son, so I was almost as respectable as I could bear to be. And I had published a novel. It was a book for adults, and so bad was it that I've never admitted its existence until now, and I'm not going to say what it was called. But it taught me that getting published wasn't either as difficult, or as important, as I'd thought. Far more difficult, and far more important, was to write well.

I needed to decide whether or not I was going to stay in the library. I liked the work, but I would have had to get some further qualification if I wanted to be a proper librarian; and then the idea of teaching came to mind, because Jude was a teacher, and I liked what she told me about it. So I went to Weymouth College of Education for a year and became a qualified teacher myself, and then looked for a job. Where should we go? Where would we like to live? There was a job advertised in Oxford; I applied and got it, and we've lived here ever since.

25

———≈•◇•≈———

In this short autobiography I haven't got the space to write about the thousand things that interest, delight, amaze, sadden, baffle, infuriate, or anger me. If I had the space I'd say something about the wholesale and vicious destruction of the public services in this country that's taken place over the past few years: especially that of education. If I were still a teacher and tried to do now the work I did for twelve years or so—and did well, I think—not only would I be discouraged, I would be forbidden. We now have a National Curriculum that lays down exactly what all children should be taught, and when they should be taught it, and insists on regular pencil-and-paper tests which seem to be checking on the pupils, but whose real purpose is to check on the teachers.

When I was teaching, I was free to decide what I should do and how I should do it, and one of the things I decided was that the pupils in my classes should learn about Greek mythology. So I began to tell them stories about the gods and heroes. I had to find good versions to work from, because I wanted to get the stories right; I didn't want to simply *read* to my pupils, I wanted to stand up and tell them the stories face-to-face. So I used Robert Graves's two-volume version of the Greek myths, which was the fullest I could find; and the *Iliad* and the *Odyssey* in the Penguin prose translation.

I worked out a course that lasted a year. In the first term I'd deal with the births and origins of the gods and goddesses, and their natures and deeds, to use Graves's phrase, and tell some of the stories about Theseus, Jason, Oedipus, Perseus, Heracles, and the other heroes; in the second term I'd start with the origins of the Trojan War and then do Homer's *Iliad* from start to finish; and in the third term I'd tell the *Odyssey*.

It was important to *tell*, not read, so I had to prepare the stories thoroughly. I taught three separate classes of twelve- and thirteen-year-olds, so I'd tell each story three times in a week; and I taught for twelve years, so I must have told each story thirty-six times. The result is that now I have all those stories entirely clear in my head, from beginning to end, and I can call them up whenever I want to.

(I did this once on holiday. We ate our evening meal in a restaurant, and my younger son, Tom, was finding it hard to sit still while we waited for the waitress to bring us the food, so I told him the *Odyssey* as a serial to keep him quiet. On the last night, when I got to that wonderful climax where Odysseus, disguised as a beggar, finally reaches his palace after twenty years away, to find it infested with rivals all seeking to marry his wife Penelope; and is recognised by his old nurse because of the scar on his leg; and gets Penelope to offer to marry any of the rivals who can string the bow of her husband, but no one can; and then Odysseus himself asks to try, and they all jeer at the ragged old beggar, but he picks up the bow and flexes it and with one easy movement slips the string into the notch and then plucks it like a harp, sending a clear note into the shocked silence of the hall. . . . Well, when I got to that, Tom, who'd been holding a drink in both hands, suddenly *bit* a large piece out of the glass in his excitement, shocking the waitress so much that she dropped the tray with our meal on it, and causing a sensation throughout the restaurant. And I sent up a silent prayer of thanks to Homer.)

Now as with my brother in Australia, the real beneficiary of all that storytelling wasn't so much the audience as the storyteller. I'd chosen—for what I thought, and think still, were good educational reasons—to do something that, by a lucky chance, was the best possible training for me as a writer. To tell great stories over and over and over again, testing and refining the language and observing the reactions of the listeners and gradually improving the timing and the rhythm and the pace, was to undergo an apprenticeship that probably wasn't very different, essentially, from the one Homer himself underwent three thousand years ago. And the more I think about it the more grateful I am for the freedom that allowed me to think about what would be best for my pupils and to design a course that provided it. I wouldn't be allowed to do it now.

And meanwhile, of course, I was writing my three pages every day. Late at night, usually. I wrote an adult novel called *Galatea,* which was published in 1978—a book I can't categorise, because it isn't really fantasy or science fiction, but it certainly isn't realistic. Nobody else was sure about it either; most reviewers were puzzled or indifferent, though some found things to praise. I'm still proud of it.

But *Galatea* was my last adult book, because I'd found that being a teacher also meant that I could write and produce school plays. Again, I couldn't do that now. I would be overwhelmed with paperwork and with all the laborious and deadening mechanisms of testing, and I simply wouldn't have the energy or the inclination. But in those days it was still possible to do things because you enjoyed them, and I enjoyed doing school plays so much that I've written for children ever since.

The first children's novel I wrote was an adaptation of a story I'd done originally as a play. It was called *Count Karlstein.* I've rewritten it since then as a picture book, so it's had three incarnations. Maybe one day it'll be a T-shirt.

The cover to
Count Karlstein
(Dell Yearling)

The cover to **The Ruby in the Smoke**
(Dell Laurel-Leaf)

The next book I did was *The Ruby in the Smoke.* The origin of that goes back to when I worked in the library in London. There was an antique shop nearby where one day I bought a couple of Victorian postcards, photographs illustrating a sentimental poem called "Daddy," showing a little girl sitting on the lap of a man dressed as a workman. The idea is that the girl's mother is dead, and they're both sad about it; in the second picture you can see Mummy looking down from Heaven, dressed like an angel. I bought these two postcards for a few pence and kept them on my desk for years without thinking very much about them, until one day I found myself wondering about the people in them, and especially about the other important person, the one who isn't visible: the photographer.

And little by little a story began to develop in my mind, and the characters in the photograph came alive and told me their names, and the photographer emerged from behind the camera so that I could see him; and somewhere in the background, coming towards the studio, was a girl of sixteen or so, in terrible trouble.

That was all I had to begin with. Stories often start in that way: not with a theme but with a picture. An intriguing, puzzling picture, like something out of a dream, with scraps of intense emotion still clinging that seem to have no reason for their intensity. I write to find out more about the picture. For that reason I seldom make a plan before I start a novel. When I hear teachers telling their pupils that they must always make a plan before beginning a story, I want to hit them. In my experience making a plan first kills a story stone dead.

So I begin to write knowing that a lot of what I write—many of those three pages a day—will probably be thrown away or abandoned, because I won't know what shape the story should take till I've finished it. But I never think of it as provisional, a first draft, because, for the same reason, I don't know what's going to be important and what isn't. You have to simultaneously take the most craftsmanlike care with every sentence *and* be ruthlessly ready to cut most of it out.

That's a state of mind I've found very hard to explain to nonwriters. Often people who don't write have a mechanistic idea of the process: They think it goes through a series of precisely defined stages, beginning with "Get an idea," proceeding through "Write first draft," and ending with "Revise and polish." Well, it's not like that at all. The writing process is much more like what goes on inside a chrysalis when a caterpillar changes into a butterfly. The parts of the caterpillar aren't unbolted one by one and reassembled in a different order according to a manual: The entire substance breaks down into a sort of soup, and gradually a butterfly comes together, something utterly different. Writing is like butterfly soup. Everything takes place at the same time, or rather outside time altogether. You're trying different titles at the same time as balancing the rhythm of this sentence with the one that comes after it and looking up the precise meaning of *vituperative* and wondering how to get rid of the murderer's accomplice and reading doubtfully over the first page and reading with pleasure over that good page in chapter 7 and thinking that if you brought in the old woman at the very beginning it would be much more effective when she turns up later and finding out whether the heroine could have caught a train to Portsmouth before eight o'clock in the morning and wondering again about the harsh tone of the ending you first thought of . . . all at once: butterfly soup.

And what's more, you can't talk about it. If you slice open a chrysalis to see what's going on, you kill the butterfly before it's formed. So all this wondering and thinking has got to take place on your own in silence and in a sort of half-light of doubt and hesitation and uncertainty, among shadows that might become solid and might dissolve again into nothing. You have to become used to this twilight world if you're going to be a writer, and some people find it difficult to do that; they need the certainty of clear light and hard facts.

With *The Ruby in the Smoke* I think I first found my voice as a children's author. And I enjoyed the setting and the characters so much that I wrote a sequel, *The Shadow in the North,* and then a third book, *The Tiger in the Well;* and I've just finished the last in the sequence. The first three books had as their main character that sixteen-year-old girl who was coming towards the photographer's studio, looking for help, and I gave the books similar titles because they were all about her. The last book, though, is called *The Tin Princess.* It has a different kind of title because the main character this time is the little girl on the man's knee in the postcard photograph I bought all those years ago when I worked in the library. I think it's the best thing I've written; but then I always think that about my most recent book.

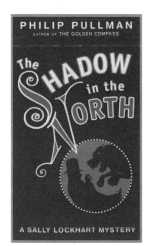

The cover to **The Shadow in the North** *(Dell Laurel-Leaf).*

29

The cover to **The Tiger in the Well** *(Dell Yearling)*

The cover to **The Tin Princess** *(Dell Laurel-Leaf)*

So now I'm halfway through my life.

What do I do?

Most importantly, my three pages a day, in my shed at the bottom of the garden. It's warm and dry in here, and full of books. And pictures, and masks, and little statues of various gods and goddesses, and a guitar and a saxophone, and a mound of artificial flowers covering my word processor, and a thousand other bits and pieces. I need colour and light and plenty of things to look at and fiddle with when I write; and silence.

Two days a week I teach at Westminster College just outside Oxford. It's a job I enjoy a lot. I teach three courses: one on the Victorian novel, so I'm working with great masterpieces; one on the traditional tale, so I'm able to work with masterpieces of a different kind, fairy tales and myths; and one on writing. Can you teach writing? There are times when I wonder if I ought to, because it's such a mysterious process and I know so little about it. I try to work like an editor: my students bring me their work and I suggest ways of making it more effective. And I enjoy the contact with them; my students are a very varied group of people, and they've all got something to say. And I like seeing my colleagues every so often and exchanging gossip. Writing has to be solitary, but I don't want to be a hermit.

And after many years I'm learning to draw properly. I want to draw figures, so that I can illustrate my own stories. I'm still just as excited by comics as I was all those years ago when I first saw Superman in Australia, and at the back of my mind I've got an idea that would only work in the form of a comic book, or a graphic novel as we're now allowed to call them; but I do need to draw it myself. After long and hard work I can now draw bodies pretty well, but I can't manage faces yet, and you need faces to tell stories with, so I keep practising and learning.

I haven't said much about my family. That's partly because they're too close to be spoken about easily, and partly because we're changing and developing all the time, and what I say now might not be true by the time this is published; but that's true of photographs, after all, and we look back on those and say, "So *that* was what we looked like then. . . . I remember!"

So, as of April 1993 Jude is studying to become a hypnotherapist. She is a healer: I've always known that, but she hasn't been sure what path to take until recently. She's the sort of person who can't stand at a bus stop for two minutes without someone pouring out his or her troubles to her. She seems to radiate some kind of sympathy beam that makes people confide in her and feel better for it, but she's never been sure that she ought to give that sort of help professionally, despite my urging her to for years. However, having looked at many different kinds of therapy, she's decided that this is the one she wants to take up. I'm sure she's right.

And she's the first and best critic of my work. If she approves of something, I know it's all right. Our older son, Jamie, is a music student. He began on the violin, but he now studies the viola at the Royal College of Music. When he was a little boy I used to take him sausage hunting in the woods. I'd hide some sausages in various places—hollow trees, bushes, empty birds' nests—and we'd go and hunt them down. He was convinced he could see their tracks, and I'd say, "That hole in the tree over there—that's the kind of place wild sausages like to hide in. Go and have a look." And he'd find them triumphantly and we'd make a fire and cook them.

Now he lives in a basement in London and comes home every few weeks to eat all the pizza in the house, sleep for eighteen hours, and go off to play in a concert somewhere. He's not a soloist; he likes the social life of an orchestra. He's far more sociable than I ever was, and I admire him a great deal.

Tom is eleven now. He's a musician too—he plays the piano and the trumpet—but mainly he's interested in science. Actually, like me, he's interested in almost everything. He and I play language games. We can speak North Martian, and we're making progress with Frog, though that's a more difficult language; there are only three words in it, though it's capable of saying much more complicated things than English. For that reason it's impossible to translate. Tom is one of the quickest and cleverest people I've ever met, and he laughs at my jokes, so he has exquisite taste as well.

Are animals part of a family? Of course they are, if you love them. I was appalled and horrified when, three months ago, I drove over our cat. He's recovered now (it seems that you can inflict much more damage on a cat than on a human being), but for days I went about haunted by guilt, though I couldn't have prevented the accident. Mouldy is ten years old, and eccentric and short-sighted and grumpy; but when I'm lying on the sofa in my usual position and he comes to sit on my chest and rub his face against mine, I feel a wave of great affection pass between us, and I think how privileged I am that an animal comes this close and trusts me.

So that's where I've come from, and where I am now. As for where I'm going, some of that is butterfly soup, and I can't talk about it. But I can say that one thing I want to do is write another book for adults and use my *Galatea* voice again. Being a writer of children's books has great advantages: It means that I can turn from a science-fiction novel to a funny short picture book to a long complex historical novel to a contemporary thriller, and my readers don't mind a bit, and my publishers don't say, "Oh, but you can't write *that!* You're a historical novelist! If you want to write something else, you'll have to use a pseudonym!" Writers of adult books don't have that freedom. But they do get a lot more attention. I'm tired of being patronised by people who think that writing for children is easy, or not really serious, or not worthy of an adult's respect. If you want to be taken seriously, it seems that you have to write for adults; and I do want to be taken seriously.

And I'm going to take some time to think about the curious and complicated relationship there is between words and pictures. Many people have written about this, but I seem to keep seeing things that other people haven't mentioned; so either I'm imagining them, or I'm onto something new. The only way to find out is to write about it.

And finally, till my dying day, I'm going to go on thinking about stories and the mysterious power they have. Earlier on I mentioned a fairy story called "The Juniper Tree." I've known that story and told it many times and been haunted by it for years, but only now do I see one reason for its hold over me. The father eating his son and saying, "I have the feeling this all belongs to me!" is a horrible image, but think of it like this: the child is symbolically the father, the father's childhood. I said I felt like that when I thought about storytelling, and now I see that when I write stories I'm consuming the experience I had as a child: my own childhood. At the end of "The Juniper Tree," the child is miraculously restored to life, and father and daughter and little boy go hand in hand into their house together, made whole again.

Of course, that only happens in stories. But that's just another way of saying that only stories can make it happen. Sometimes I can hardly believe my luck.

Philip Pullman
Oxford, England

Tim Kirk

Gallivespian Spy

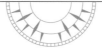

The Literary Influences on Pullman's His Dark Materials

I HAVE STOLEN IDEAS FROM EVERY BOOK I HAVE EVER READ. . . . BUT THERE ARE THREE DEBTS THAT NEED ACKNOWLEDGMENT ABOVE ALL THE REST. ONE IS TO THE ESSAY "ON THE MARIONETTE THEATRE," BY HEINRICH VON KLEIST . . . THE SECOND IS TO JOHN MILTON'S *PARADISE LOST*. THE THIRD IS TO THE WORKS OF WILLIAM BLAKE.

—Acknowledgments in *The Amber Spyglass*

n his website, Philip Pullman answers an oft-asked question posed to all writers of fiction: Where do you get your ideas? His response: "[T]he important thing is not just having the idea—it's writing the book. That's the difficult thing, the thing that takes the time and the energy and the discipline. The initial idea is much less important, actually, than what you do with it."

The initial ideas for His Dark Materials came from an essay by Heinrich von Kleist, Milton's *Paradise Lost,* and William Blake's *Songs of Innocence and of Experience.*

"ON THE MARIONETTE THEATRE"

Heinrich von Kleist (1777–1811) wrote in an essay titled "On the Marionette Theatre" that as we become more self-aware, we lose our natural grace, but that it can be regained through knowledge and experience. It's the opposite of what Christians believe, that we are creatures of sin, that we are fallen and can only rise to a state of grace after being *forgiven* for our sins, at which point God may *choose* to bless us with his grace.

Both Kleist and Pullman believe that grace can be attained by hard work and knowledge, and that because it's a state we arrive at through our own efforts, it's superior to the innate grace we enjoyed as children. That notion is central to His Dark Materials: We eat from the tree of knowledge and are not cursed but blessed. Knowledge is not mankind's damnation but our salvation.

In His Dark Materials, Lyra sheds her innocence by learning, by growing into knowledge; and although she naturally and intuitively knows how to read the complicated Alethiometer without any formal training, she will over time lose that natural skill. However, she's told that years of hard work will restore it; moreover, she will be more skilled at reading it because she will have earned it.

As Pullman asserts, this learning experience is the closest we can come to evolving toward a godlike state of regaining grace through our own efforts. Also, Pullman reminds us, we should not put all of our hopes and dreams in an afterlife that he doesn't believe exists; we should live in the here and now, enjoy and celebrate our physical world with all its beauty and wonder, and realize this is the only life we can ever know and experience.

A contrary vision, Pullman advocates surety over uncertainty: We *know* we are here on Earth, so why not make the most of it? Why yearn and pine for an otherworldly existence that you don't, and *can't*, know exists except on the basis of faith? Given Pullman's deeply held convictions, His Dark Materials could only have been written by an atheist. (Playing the devil's advocate: What, one wonders, would he have written if he were of the Christian faith?)

JOHN MILTON AND *PARADISE LOST*

Because John Milton's epic poem *Paradise Lost* is not essential reading to understanding His Dark Materials, most people will never tackle it.

But knowing what *Paradise Lost* is about gives us an appreciation of what Pullman has accomplished in His Dark Materials.

The Norton Anthology of English Literature (Vol. 1) explains that *Paradise Lost* is an epic poem written in 1667 in which Milton "gives us love, war, supernatural characters, a descent into Hell, a catalogue of warriors, all the conventional items of epic machinery."

Written in English heroic verse without rhyme (more commonly called blank verse), the poem is approximately 80,000 words; but even in its day, according to *Norton,* "many readers found the poem hard going" and "the printer asked Milton for some prose 'Arguments' or summary explanations of the action in the various books, and prefixed them to later issues of the poem."

The "Argument" for book one (of twelve) summarizes it thus:

> The first book proposes, first in brief, the whole subject, man's disobedience, and the loss thereupon of Paradise, wherein he was placed: then touches the prime cause of his fall, the serpent, or rather Satan in the serpent; who, revolting from God, and drawing to his side many legions of angels, was, by the command of God, driven out of Heaven, with all his crew, into the great deep.

In an introduction commissioned especially for a new Oxford Press edition of *Paradise Lost,* Pullman recounts a story told to him by a correspondent, in which a "semi-literate, ageing country squire" is read the story of *Paradise Lost;* after hearing it, the squire exclaimed, "By God! I know not what the outcome may be, but this Lucifer is a damned fine fellow, and I hope he may win!"

An illustrated edition of Milton's **Paradise Lost,** *with an introduction by Philip Pullman*

Pullman, who obviously has sympathy for the devil, felt that Milton—then an old man, embittered and blind—was on the right track: In the epic poem, Satan muses as to why God had warned Adam and Eve against eating from the Tree of Forbidden Knowledge, knowing full well that His admonition will be tempting precisely because of its forbidden nature. Why, Satan ponders, is ignorance a preferable state to knowledge? What's the sense in that? Why, Satan concludes, there's *no* sense!

Though Milton had said that his epic poem justifies the ways of God to mankind, it does exactly the opposite: It builds a strong case for the devil's point of view, that God's selfishness is at the heart of His prohibition. As Pullman writes in his introduction:

> Suppose that the prohibition on the knowledge of good and evil were an expression of jealous cruelty, and the gaining of such knowledge an act of virtue? Suppose the Fall should be celebrated and not deplored? As I played with it, my story resolved itself into an account of the necessity of growing up, and a refusal to lament the loss of innocence. The true end of human life, I found myself saying, was not redemption by a nonexistent Son of God, but the gaining and transmission of wisdom. Innocence is not wise, and wisdom cannot be innocent, and if we are going to do any good in the world, we have to leave childhood behind.

This is at the heart of His Dark Materials. In order for Lyra to grow into adulthood, she *must* leave her childhood behind. She cannot forever remain innocent and free: She must achieve experience and learn from it, accumulate wisdom, and grow into adulthood. It's that wisdom that changes not only her, but countless other worlds as well.

Pullman notes in an afterword to *Paradise Lost* that there are several annotated editions in print, so that "no one who wants to explore further need do so without expert guidance." For those who can guide themselves, the Oxford edition with the Pullman introduction is a good place to start. It's a handsome book with outstanding production values: paper stock, typography, and design are all first-rate. This illustrated edition belongs on the shelf of any serious Pullman reader.

WILLIAM BLAKE

Blake, who lived from 1757 to 1827, received formal training only in art; nevertheless, he's rightly considered to have had "visionary gifts, as a painter, engraver and poet," as Richard Holmes noted in the Folio Society edition of William Blake's *Songs of Innocence and of Experience: Shewing the Two Contrary States of the Human Soul,* published in 1992.

***William Blake's* Songs of Innocence and of Experience**

Though well known and celebrated in literary circles today, Blake's *Songs of Innocence and of Experience* was not celebrated much at all in his time. According to Holmes, "less than thirty copies are known to have been sold in his lifetime."

The first half of the book is comprised of poems that celebrate the state of innocence; the second half, experience. It is in the second half that we find poems 34 ("The Little Girl Lost") and 35 ("The Little Girl Found"), about a young girl named Lyca—similar in name and in Pullman's own description of Lyra, in *The Subtle Knife,* as "a little girl, lost."

In fact, we also find other significant references to Lyca: poems 13 and 14 ("The Little Boy Lost" and "The Little Boy Found"), and poems 50 and 51 ("A Little Boy Lost" and "A Little Girl Lost").

Pullman found in William Blake a kindred spirit, another Devil's advocate. Like Pullman, Blake found himself at odds with the basic tenets of Christianity. As *The Norton Anthology of English Literature* (Vol. 2, revised) explains, Blake's *The Marriage of Heaven and Hell* is "an onslaught against the timidly conventional and self-righteous members of society, as well as against many of the stock opinions of orthodox Christian piety and morality."

39

The critical—and to some, heretical and blasphemous—views shared by Pullman and Blake can be summed up in a line from *The Marriage of Heaven and Hell*: "The reason [John] Milton wrote in fetters when he wrote of Angels & God, and at liberty when of Devils & Hell, is because he was a true Poet and of the Devil's party without knowing it."

Pullman, in several interviews, alludes to this line and is quick to tell his interviewers that, like Blake, he is also of the Devil's party—but he knows it. Unapologetic and unrepentant, Pullman is adamant that His Dark Materials is, like the principal work that inspired it, an assault against our preconceived notions and sensibilities that blind us to the truth: that in order to realize our human potential, we must grow and learn instead of blindly accepting religious dogma that keeps us in fetters. Ignorance, says Pullman, is paradise lost, but knowledge is paradise regained.

"The Little Girl Lost," a poem by William Blake in The Marriage of Heaven and Hell *(The girl's name is Lyca—similar to Lyra)*

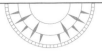

What Does "His Dark Materials" Refer To?

It specifically refers to *Paradise Lost,* Book II, line 916:

> *Into this wild abyss*
> *The womb of nature, and perhaps her grave,*
> *Of neither sea, nor shore, nor air, nor fire,*
> *But all these in their pregnant causes mixed*
> *Confusedly, and which thus must ever fight,*
> *Unless the almighty maker them ordain*
> *His dark materials to create more worlds,*
> *Into this wild abyss the wary fiend*
> *Stood on the brink of hell and looked a while,*
> *Pondering his voyage . . .* [emphasis mine]

n an introduction to the Oxford edition to *Paradise Lost,* Pullman said that he first encountered, and fell in love with, the poem after his English teacher, Miss Enid Jones, introduced him to it. Pullman loved its language and its rhythm.

Pullman has on numerous occasions—in interviews for the print and electronic media, in online discussions, and in public forums—made no bones about the considerable debt he owes John Milton. What Pullman does in His Dark Materials is justify the ways of Satan to man. As Pullman explained: "As I played with it, my story resolved itself into an account of the necessity of growing up, and a refusal to lament the loss of innocence. The true end of human life . . . [is] the gaining and transmission of wisdom."

———⟨∻⟩———

Pullman's interpretation, then, is not only a celebration of, but a justification for, Milton's thesis that, far from being damned for his actions, Lucifer should be praised.

It's a view that has put Pullman at odds with the Christian community, which refuses to justify the ways of Pullman to the reading community at large. Perhaps even more galling to Christians, His Dark Materials has enjoyed a large, worldwide audience that shows every sign of increasing with each passing year.

I suspect that Pullman has renewed people's interest in John Milton, at least among the academically inclined, although *Paradise Lost* is admittedly not light fare.

Paradise Lost is beautifully written with striking imagery, which is why Pullman, in his introduction to the book, said it had "the power to stir a physical response" in him.

No question, *Paradise Lost,* originally published in 1667, is a magnificent achievement, all the more remarkable because its author wrote it under difficult and trying circumstances. *The Norton Anthology* notes that he wrote it "in blindness, poverty, defeat, and relative isolation."

Paradise Lost has stood the test of time; so, too, will His Dark Materials.

PART 2

POINTING THE WAY
TO THE BOOKS OF
HIS DARK MATERIALS:
*THE GOLDEN COMPASS,
THE SUBTLE KNIFE, AND
THE AMBER SPYGLASS*

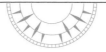

DISCOVERING PHILIP PULLMAN'S UNIVERSE

he polar bear with very humanlike, intelligent eyes stared directly at me. Riding on his massive back of thick white fur, a young girl is bundled up against the arctic cold, accompanied by a small brown mouse.

The illustration on the cover of the book jacket had certainly caught my attention. Its title: *The Golden Compass*. What, I thought, does that mean? What does it refer to? Its author: Philip Pullman, a name with which I was not familiar.

A children's book, I thought. Probably filled with homilies and lessons to impart and a decidedly cheery and upbeat ending. As to the plot, the Library of Congress Cataloging-in-Publication Data summarized it: "Accompanied by her dæmon, Lyra Belacqua sets out to prevent her best friend and other kidnapped children from becoming the subjects of gruesome experiments in the Far North."

Pretty bare bones, I thought. Probably standard fantasy fare. But distracted by hordes of children—tourists, mostly, who travel in packs in my small corner of the world, Colonial Williamsburg—I put the book down and didn't encounter Philip Pullman again until years later, when it was

Pantalaimon as a mouse

clear that the book I had overlooked was no stereotypical children's book or standard fantasy but an important book in its own right.

As it turned out, Pullman's first novel in the His Dark Materials series would rack up a long list of awards, both in the United Kingdom, where it had been published as *Northern Lights,* and in the United States, where it had been published under the curious title of *The Golden Compass.*

Its proud U.S. publisher, Random House, commented that the book "is considered one of the best juvenile fantasy novels of the past 20 years."

The second time around, I bought the book, thinking that I'd dip into it at my leisure; I'd read a few chapters and finish it a few months later, but I was hooked after reading the first line of the book: "Lyra and her dæmon moved through the darkening hall, taking care to keep to one side, out of sight of the kitchen."

I stayed up late, well into the early morning hours, and finished it in one sitting. I was smitten. This was no juvenile novel, at least not in the sense that it was written only for kids: Clearly, adults would also be swept away by Pullman's powerful storytelling engine. This was also a novel that, unfortunately, would be branded as a fantasy novel, which meant people were likely to confuse it with books populated with elves, hobbits, dragons, and other mythical beings.

Both "children's book" and "fantasy," I felt, were unfortunate labels for Pullman's novel because they might cause adults to overlook it and by doing so do the book and the author a grave disservice.

To put it simply, *The Golden Compass* was one of the best books I had read in a long time, and it whetted my appetite for the other two books in the series, *The Subtle Knife* and *The Amber Spyglass.*

I thought to myself: *Christians will be outraged when they hear about this book . . .* and they were, of course, attacking Pullman in print where possible because he dared to frame the question of God's existence in a book that reached millions of impressionable young children who, they feared, might take his message to heart, or at least start asking unanswerable questions about the Christian deity that have confounded theologians for centuries, such as why God stands idly by while humankind suffers unremitting pain.

No wonder a British columnist characterized Pullman as "the most dangerous author in Britain," concluding that Pullman is "semi-satanic."

Pullman, in fact, is neither. As a writer and an individual, he is entitled to his own convictions, even when they are contrary to the prevailing theological opinion that the *promise* of an afterlife is better than the reality of what we have here on Earth.

After discussing the book idea with his U.K. editor David Fickling, who responded enthusiastically to his overtures, Pullman retired to a small, modestly outfitted shed in his backyard where, on a daily basis for the next seven years, he would laboriously write pages in longhand on lined notebook paper and bring to life his cast of characters: Lyra and her dæmon Pantalaimon (Pan, for short), her star-crossed parents (Mrs. Coulter and Lord Asriel), and Iorek, a magnificent polar bear who, like Lyra, eventually finds his own way back home. Propelled by a story-telling engine that engages the reader's attention and won't let go, His Dark Materials is pure narrative genius, storytelling at its finest.

The day after I read *The Golden Compass,* I called a good friend of mine, Tim Kirk, whose opinion about books I value. When I brought up the subject, Tim—a former Disney Imagineer, illustrator, and fan of imaginative fiction—summed up my feelings exactly: "It's the best book I've read since *The Lord of the Rings.*"

I told him I agreed.

The next morning, I was back at the bookstore, where I bought *The Subtle Knife* and *The Amber Spyglass,* thankful that I didn't have to wait a year for *The Subtle Knife* to be published and two years after that for *The Amber Spyglass* to be published (as had readers of *The Golden Compass* in 1996).

As I had with *The Golden Compass,* I raced through the books. Afterward, I thought to myself that Pullman, a fiercely intelligent writer who prefers to let his stories and not himself take center stage, had gone where angels fear to tread: criticizing the Church that has had a tena-cious hold over millions of people—true believers and nonbelievers alike—for centuries.

It's now twelve years after the original publication of *Northern Lights* (aka *The Golden Compass*) and the fans, critics, and academicians have affirmed what I felt was so obvious when reading it and the two books that followed: that here was a story filled with wonder and awe, that here were characters (Lyra, Mrs. Coulter, Lord Asriel, Iorek Byrnison, and others) that captured my imagination, and that here were dæmons, witches, and monstrous creatures aplenty.

What more could any reader ask for?

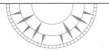

Visualizing the Technology in Lyra's World

By Tim Kirk

he task of a production designer for film is to take an author's vision and translate it into a living reality—a virtual, convincing environment for the film's characters to inhabit and play out their stories. It must possess a logical structure; it must feel "right," and it must provide a compelling framework for the action of the film. The best films—from *Intolerance* and *Metropolis*, to *Gone with the Wind* and *Citizen Kane*, to *Blade Runner, Pirates of the Caribbean,* and *Spiderman*—all owe a large part of their success to the work of the production designer.

Naphtha Lamp

When I illustrate a work of fiction, my task is very similar: to be true to the author's vision and to pay close attention to description and detail, while at the same time bringing my own interpretation to the work. A vast amount of painstaking research—combined with imagination and the ability to extrapolate—is invariably involved.

The Golden Compass initially takes place in another dimension, a world parallel to our own: Lyra's world. It is a world that would seem familiar to us in many ways, but vastly different in others. Lyra's era seems equivalent to our own late nineteenth to early twentieth century; say, 1890 to 1920 or so. Electricity ("anbaric force"), the internal combustion engine, and steam power are all widely employed, with the addition of some form of atomic power ("atomcraft") . . . and a strong supernatural/mystical element provides an interesting counterpoint to the technology. This helped me to set the "look" of that world: industrial, civic, and domestic architecture is based on Victorian and

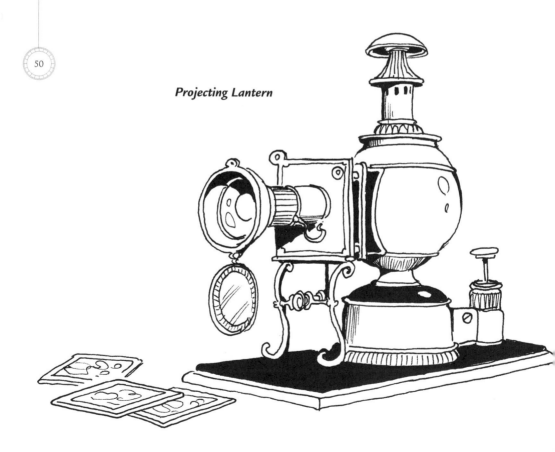

Projecting Lantern

Gyptian Narrowboat

Edwardian era prototypes; canal boats, steamships, and airships (zeppelins, gyropters, etc.) have had equivalents in our world—my interpretations are recognizably of the period, with subtle variations. When it comes to out-and-out fantasy—say, cliff-ghasts, Gallevespians, Spectres, or armored bears—I have the author's descriptions as a starting point. This is particularly important when the subject matter is something new and original, and not a stock fantasy prop like an elf or dragon.

Steamer

51

Anbaric Park

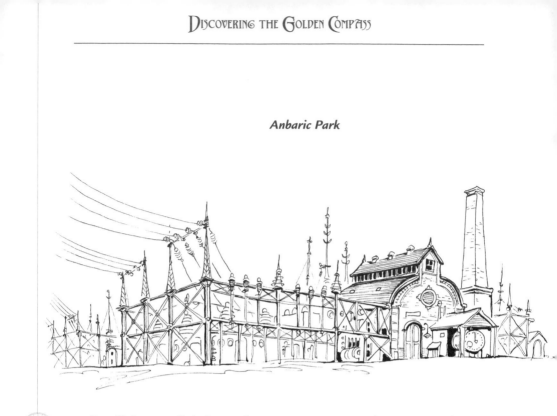

In all issues of design—character, costume, architecture, technology—I think it's very important that the illustrator always turn first to the original author of the work, and not be too swayed by other versions of that world that have appeared previously: other illustrators' visions, film, game media, comic art, or whatever.

Atomcraft Works

Gyropters

These all may be valid interpretations, but they're not the illustrator's interpretations. Simply copying a character portrait from a film shot is not accomplishing much, creatively. What I'm advocating is a direct dialogue between writer and artist; a conversation, if you will—a true meeting of minds.

53

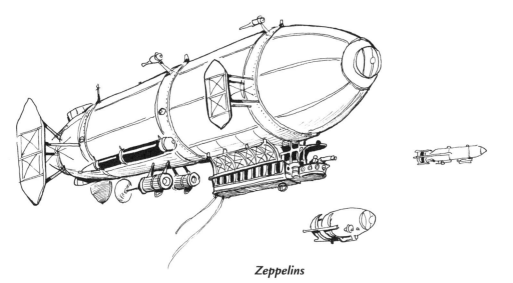

Zeppelins

A re-creation of the wrapper from a bar of chocolatl,
a one-of-a-kind artifact created by Tiffany Vincent

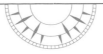

Pointing the Way
to His Dark Materials

About His Dark Materials

 hree books comprise His Dark Materials: *The Golden Compass, The Subtle Knife,* and *The Amber Spyglass.* Each will be discussed in chronological order.

Non-Spoiler Alert!

I have on my shelves virtually every book in print about Philip Pullman and His Dark Materials, in addition to study guides and hundreds of pages of analyses from the Internet.

The one thing they all have in common is that they presume the reader has *already* read the books in question. While this may be true of many, especially those in the academic community, the fact remains that new readers do not want a detailed plot synopsis because it ruins the reading experience for them. Storytelling, as Pullman noted, is about "what happens next?" So if you already know what comes next, what incentive is there to read on?

Given that concern, I've decided to dispense with the detailed plot summary and talk about the book and some of the key concepts therein. I'll lightly sketch in the plot, to get you oriented, and provide an overview of the key characters, places, and things so that you'll know who's who and what's what. I'll try to minimize the spoilers insofar as possible, as well.

Stephen King, when asked what he deliberately avoids reading, said he rarely reads science fiction because he doesn't want to learn a new vocabulary just to read a book. The same problem exists, to some degree, with a series like His Dark Materials with its fantasy settings, though in this instance, a lot of the words sound similar to our own (chocolatl = chocolate). However, the people, places, and things are sometimes strikingly different; for example, in our world, our souls are internal, but in Lyra's world, souls are external and have physical form in the shape of animals. But once you know who the key characters, places, and things are, it's easy to understand what's happening in the story. I have therefore provided an abbreviated listing to help orient newcomers to Pullman's universe. (A detailed listing, beyond the scope of this book, can be found in Laurie Frost's excellent and indispensable resource, *The Elements of His Dark Materials,* which arranges topics thematically and then alphabetically; a more abbreviated listing is available in *Dark Matters* by Lance Parkin and Mark Jones.)

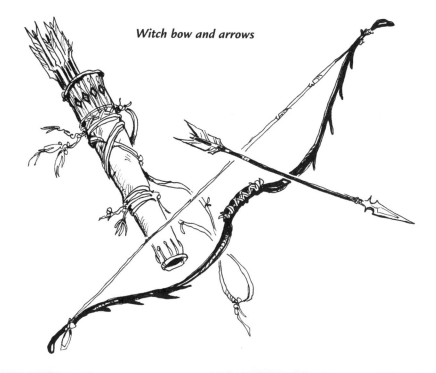

Witch bow and arrows

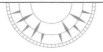

THE GOLDEN COMPASS

(U.K. edition, *Northern Lights*)

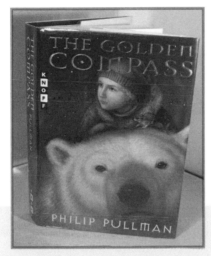

*Published in 1996
by Alfred A. Knopf*

Cover art by Eric Rohmann

*Available in hardback, trade
paperback, paperback, and
unabridged audiobook on
compact disc*

Jacket copy: "Lyra Belacqua is content to run wild among the scholars of Jordan College, with her dæmon familiar, Pantalaimon, always by her side. When her uncle, Lord Asriel, returns from the north with tales of mystery and danger, it seems to have little to do with her—even the rumor of the severed child. But his visit sets off a chain of events that draws Lyra into the heart of a terrible struggle—a struggle that involves scientists performing hideous experiments on children, alliances with Gyptians and witch clans, battles with trained mercenaries, and armored bears. And through it all, there dawns in Lyra a sense that her success or failure may mean even more than simply life or death."

The book's front flap copy is deliberately vague and raises more questions than it answers, mentioning Lyra's quest north but carefully avoiding all mention of the alethiometer and Dust, both central to the storyline.

The Golden Compass is set in an alternate world very similar, and yet dissimilar, to our own in many ways. Lyra's world is a cross between Victorian England and our world, but clearly set in our time frame. Some examples of contrasts and comparisons between Lyra's world and our world are:

Lyra: anbaric power (vs. electrical)
Lyra: hand-delivered mail only (vs. e-mail)
Lyra: lodestone resonator (vs. telegraph)
Lyra: photogram (vs. photograph)
Lyra: projecting lantern (vs. slide film and digitized images shown on large computer screens)
Lyra: typewriter (vs. computer)
Lyra: phones with cranks (vs. touchtone and cellular phones)

Transportation: Lyra's world has trains, boats, balloons, gyropters (think helicopters), and zeppelins.

Weaponry: Lyra's world has pistols, rifles, and bombs, including a napalm-like bomb, and a more sophisticated bomb that uses DNA to identify its victim. Lyra's world also has an abundance of more primitive weaponry, such as swords, arrows, crossbows, and catapults.

Lyra's world has supernatural beings: angels, talking bears, flying witches, ghosts, cliff-ghasts, tiny people called Gallivespians, and others too numerous to mention. But by far the most striking dissimilarity between Lyra's world and ours is that in her world, each person has a

Unabridged audio recording of the 10th anniversary edition of The Golden Compass

dæmon—his or her soul, in external form, capable of speech, with the ability to shift shapes when young.

(When we first meet Lyra's dæmon, Pantalaimon, he's in the form of a dark brown moth. Throughout *The Golden Compass,* he changes shapes as necessary, though his favorite form is an ermine, a mink-like creature.)

At the heart of *The Golden Compass* is a mysterious substance called Dust. It is Dust that commands Lord Asriel's attention, as well as that of the Scholars of Jordan College, who meet with him to discuss its presence and its implications. Dust is also the subject of great interest to the Church, which seeks to control it for nefarious purposes.

Also at the heart of *The Golden Compass,* as well as of *The Subtle Knife* and *The Amber Spyglass,* is an eleven-year-old girl named Lyra Belacqua who lives at Jordan College in Oxford, England. Previously, she lived a carefree existence, but her world drastically changes after she takes refuge in a wardrobe closet in the Retiring Room of Jordan College and overhears something that she should not. This sets into motion a chain of events that takes her far from the safe confines of Jordan College to the distant north, where she takes her first step into a brave new world.

Lyra, however, is not alone. She is assisted by Roger Parslow, her best friend; the beautiful, cultured Mrs. Coulter, who takes Lyra under her wing; John Faa, the king of the Gyptians; Farder Coram, who teaches her how to read a strange instrument known as the alethiometer; Dr. Lanselius, who introduces her to a talking bear named Iorek Byrnison; and Lee Scoresby, a Texan whose hot-air balloon proves invaluable.

Against Lyra and her friends, there is an array of powerful foes: the mysterious Gobblers who abduct children; the king of bears, Iofur Raknison; a race of men called Tartars; and the monstrous, flat-headed cliff-ghasts, leather-winged creatures with hideous frog-like facial features.

59

Pantalaimon as a moth

Most important, Lyra has one of the very few alethiometers in the world. A truth-telling device, it helps her navigate her way through a world in which it is difficult to tell friend from foe, and nearly impossible to predict what might happen, to whom, and when. The alethiometer, however, keeps Lyra on the right track, no matter who (or what) tries to distract her from her destiny.

Key Characters, Places, and Things

Characters

Alethiometrist • One who can read the alethiometer.

Asriel, Lord • A powerful man with an intimidating manner; his dæmon is a snow leopard named Stelmaria. A member of the nobility, Lord Asriel's last name is Belacqua, and he is supposedly Lyra's uncle. On the pretense that he needs funds to explore further the mysterious phenomenon called Dust, he seeks additional funding from the Scholars at Jordan; Lord Asriel's purpose, however, goes far beyond mere research. He seeks to explore new worlds and mount an assault against a formidable foe. He is no friend of the Church, which seeks to control Dust for its own nefarious purposes. Lord Asriel's manservant, Thorold, sums up his master perfectly, saying he's "not like other men."

Bears • The talking polar bears with opposable claws live in the far north, in a city called Svalbard. Fierce by nature, these bears are capable of extraordinary metalwork, which allows them to construct out of meteor rocks what they call "sky-metal." From this they fashion their body armor, which Iorek Byrnison calls his soul, his dæmon, as it were. These armored bears, who call themselves Panserbjørne, are justifiably feared, not only because of their strength, but also their speed, ferocity, intelligence, and ability to see instinctively through deception—an innate skill that Iorek tells Lyra humans lost because they have "forgotten" it. In His Dark Materials, the two bears of prominence are Iorek Byrnison and Iofur Raknison, who will find themselves locked in mortal combat.

Boreal, Lord • Sir Charles Latrom is an older man, well into his sixties, who is distinguished-looking, clearly prosperous, and lives in Will's world at Limefield House in Old Headington, though he harkens from Lyra's world, hence his real name (Lord Boreal). A clue as to his true nature: His dæmon is a serpent.

Byrnison, Iorek • In exile from his homeland, Iorek is an armored bear who is befriended by Lyra; she helps him recover his armor. In exchange, he agrees to help her on her quest north, and does so. Iorek is not typical of his race. He is legitimately a prince and his fall from greatness is tragic. When Lyra meets him, he's resigned to his lot but determined to carry out his duties and obligations in an honorable fashion. That is his way, although dishonorable humans got him drunk and took away his armor to exploit his skills in metalworking. It is Iorek who gives Lyra the name "Silvertongue" for her dangerous role in convincing the false bear king, Iofur Raknison, that she is a dæmon.

Cliff-Ghasts • Winged, mortal creatures with hooked claws, they are only three feet (or so) tall but strong and predatory by nature. Noted for their stench and their distinctive vocalization ("yowk-yowk"), these ghastly creatures live high in the cliffs (hence their name).

Coram, Farder • A highly regarded senior member of the Gyptians, he befriends Lyra and helps her understand how to read the alethiometer. His dæmon is named Sophonax ("wisdom" in Greek); she's a larger-than-normal-size cat. In his youth, he rescued the witch Serafina Pekkala from a bird attack in Eastern Anglia.

Costa, Ma • The mother of Tony and Billy Costa, she nursed Lyra as a child and, when it came time to place Lyra, she pleaded her case to assume guardianship, but it was not granted. Nonetheless, Ma Costa has kept an eagle eye on Lyra, through a spy at Jordan College. Ma Costa's dæmon is, appropriately, a hawk.

Coulter, Marisa • Most often referred to as Mrs. Coulter, she is beautiful, intelligent, and cunning—all attributes mirrored by her distinctive dæmon, an exotic, malevolent golden monkey. She seeks power, initially through her first husband (Edward Coulter); after his death she uses her formidable attributes to rise in power through the Church. She establishes the General Oblation Board that carries out experiments on children and their dæmons, utilizing a new process called intercision. The experiments are conducted in Bolvangar, in the north Arctic. She is a complex, intriguing, and obviously irresistible woman.

Dæmons • In Lyra's world, everyone has a dæmon. Perhaps inspired by the American Indian spirit guide or a familiar (an animal that serves a witch), a dæmon is a shape-shifting entity that, at puberty, "settles" and becomes fixed in form, reflecting its counterpart's true nature. The form of a dæmon varies—birds, insects, mammals—and, when its counterpart is killed, the dæmon vanishes without a trace. Similarly, if a dæmon is killed, its counterpart dies, as well. An external part of one's soul, a dæmon is inextricably linked to its counterpart in many ways. A dæmon is literally an extension of oneself. In fact, to be separated from one's dæmon causes great pain to both parties—the greater the distance, the greater the pain. Witch's dæmons, though, can be separated by great distances; their dæmons always take the form of birds.

Pullman, who is frequently asked about his dæmon, responds that his is a magpie or jackdaw, birds that are curious by nature and pick up brightly colored objects. (It's a good metaphor for a writer.)

Not surprisingly, by the time a reader finishes reading His Dark Materials, he is usually wondering what form his dæmon would take.

Faa, Lord John • He's the Lord of the western gypsies. Loyal to Lord Asriel for helping his people (the Gyptians), Lord John Faa repays Lord Asriel by keeping a watchful eye over Lyra. Faa's dæmon is a crow. After discussing the issue of abducted children with other Gyptians, he decides to lead an expedition north, to Bolvangar, to liberate them.

Gobblers • A nickname given to the people who are snatching up children and taking them north for experiments to be conducted under the auspices of the General Oblation Board (hence "GOB" of "gobblers").

Golden Monkey • Marisa Coulter's dæmon is a beautiful but deadly animal with a sadistic streak. Interestingly, the Golden Monkey has no name, the only dæmon in the story with that curious distinction. (Pullman said that whenever he tried to get near to the Golden Monkey, it frightened him and he therefore couldn't come up with its name.)

Gyptians • A tight-knit group of people who live in a community of boats; their leader is John Faa. In times of crisis, their leader calls them together for a Byanroping, a formal gathering of the families. At one such meeting, the decision is made to head north to rescue the abducted children, taken by the Gobblers.

Lyra • A headstrong, semi-feral girl who calls Jordan College her home. Her formal name is Lyra Belacqua, but she's also known (to the polar bear Iorek Byrnison) as Lyra Silvertongue because of her fluid way of lying so convincingly—an attribute that, time and again, proves useful. Eleven years old, Lyra's education is hit-and-miss since she is not receiving any formal training, which is how she prefers it. Hers is an idyllic life, climbing on rooftops, playing with her best friend, Roger Parslow, and engaging in mischief, principally against the unsuspecting townsfolk in Oxford. Her dæmon's name is Pantalaimon, whom she often calls Pan. Although His Dark Materials is the engine that powers the story, the heart of the story is Lyra and her transformation from a child to a young adult, from a state of innocence and grace to knowledge and experience, from a carefree life to one of responsibility, with extraordinary consequences.

Makarios, Tony • A boy who is beguiled by Mrs. Coulter and becomes a victim of her experiments at Bolvangar. His dæmon, Ratter, assumes the form of a rat.

Pantalaimon • Lyra's dæmon, whom she often calls Pan. We first meet him in chapter 1, in which he takes the form of a brown moth. Throughout His Dark Materials, he assumes various forms as the situation dictates. (As for Pullman's inspiration for the name, it's hard to tell, though there is a Saint Pantaleon, a martyr who refused to denounce his Christian faith and endured a series of executions, all of which failed because of divine intervention. He subsequently asked God to forgive his would-be executioners, which earned him the name Panteleimon, which means "all-compassionate.")

Parslow, Roger • Lyra's best childhood friend who works at Jordan College as a kitchen boy.

Pekkala, Serafina • The Clan-Queen of the Lapland Witches of Lake Enara, her dæmon is a beautiful goose named Kaisa. Connected to Farder Coram, she is sympathetic to Lord Asriel's mission, befriends the children incarcerated at Bolvangar, and assists Lee Scoresby and Dr. Mary Malone.

Raknison, Iofur • A prince among armored bears, he is the false king who lives in Svalbard and must do battle with Iorek Byrnison to retain his power.

Scoresby, Lee • A Texan balloonist who knows the Arctic region intimately and therefore is indispensable to Lyra and the Gyptians' trek north. His dæmon is Hester, a wiry, tough hare. (Perhaps Pullman had in mind the snowshoe hare, found in arctic North America.)

Witches • Living unusually long lives, they dwell in the northlands. Organized in clans, witches fly using branches of cloud pine. Unlike people, witches' dæmons can be separated from them by great distances without injury. A witch's dæmon is always a bird. In terms of allegiance, some assist Lord Asriel's efforts, yet others oppose him and work for the Church and its powerful elements. The witch we see most often in His Dark Materials is Serafina Pekkala.

Cloud pine branch

PLACES

Aerodock • A docking station for zeppelins, a principal means of air transportation.

Brytain • In Lyra's world, Britain.

Jordan College • In Lyra's world, the oldest, and grandest, college in Oxford, inspired by Pullman's own Exeter College in Oxford. It is Lyra's home, after she was deposited there by her parents. The college is best known for its work in experimental theology, known in Will's world as quantum physics.

Oxford • Both Lyra and Will live in their respective Oxfords. Lyra's Oxford is similar, but in many ways dissimilar, to our own, which is the Oxford that Will lives in. A longtime resident of Oxford, Pullman's intimate knowledge of the two parts of the city—town and gown—gives His Dark Materials a texture that makes Lyra's Oxford palpably real. Though the trappings of Lyra's Oxford date back to the Victorian age, its time frame is contemporary.

Svalbard • The stronghold of the armored bears, it's located in the northern regions. The area is a desolate landscape, principally mountainous. Because of its isolation, it's a favorite place to exile prisoners and dissidents. (In the real world, it's an archipelago in the Arctic Ocean, controlled by Norway.)

THINGS

Alethiometer • Also referred to as the "golden compass," this portable, mechanical hand-held device is surprisingly heavy, as Lyra discovers. It is, in essence, a symbol reader. Its face has four hands; three are fixed and one sweeps around a ring with thirty-six symbols that, when properly interpreted, tell what will happen given specific circumstances. Few in number (only a handful exist), the alethiometer takes years of intense studying and training to use properly.

Anbaric Power • From the Arabic word *anbar* (meaning "amber"), this word designates electricity in Lyra's world.

Fire-Thrower • A weapon used by the armored bears at their stronghold at Svalbard, this weapon is formidable.

Projecting Lantern • A slide projector in Lyra's world. Lord Asriel uses it to make his presentation to the Jordan scholars.

Tokay • A sweet wine from Europe, it's a favorite of Lord Asriel, who regularly visits Jordan College. The old vintages are especially prized because of their rarity and exquisite taste, and opened only for special occasions.

Zeppelin • In Lyra's world, a popular form of air transportation. In Will's world, travel by zeppelin ended in 1937 after the Hindenburg burst into flames during a mooring operation.

OTHER

Aurora Borealis • A natural phenomenon in the polar region that manifests as a shimmering curtain of multicolored lights, predominantly green, blue, and purple. A spectacular light show, it is called the northern lights because it is visible only in the northern hemisphere. (There's a similar phenomenon in the southern hemisphere called the Aurora Australis.) The Aurora Borealis is a subject of great interest to Lord Asriel.

Church • After the death of Pope Calvin, who in Lyra's world had moved his seat of power to Geneva and installed the Consistorial Court of Discipline, the Papacy was quickly abolished; in its place, a confederation of colleges, courts, and other bodies, called the Magisterium, was established. Somewhat modeled on, and perhaps inspired by, the Roman Catholic church, the Church in Lyra's world is absolute: its power unquestioned, its doctrine unchallenged. The branches of the Magisterium include the General Oblation Board and the Society of the Work of the Holy Spirit; the Imperial Guard of Muscovy is its formidable and justifiably feared military branch.

Dark Matter Research Unit • Dr. Mary Malone and Dr. Oliver Payne conduct studies on Shadow-particles (Shadows) at an Oxford college in Will's world.

Dust • Central to all three books, it makes its first appearance in the first chapter of *The Golden Compass*. The inhabitants of each of the worlds substantially visited have their own perception of Dust. Some fear it (Lyra's world, the Church), others embrace it (the Mulefa in *The Amber Spyglass*), others seek to harness its power (Mrs. Coulter and Lord Asriel), yet others merely wish to understand it (Dr. Mary Malone).

Inspired by quantum physics, with its ongoing discussion about the nature of the universe being dark matter, and referencing the Bible (Genesis 3:19, "for dust thou art, and unto dust shall thou return"), Dust is the central focus of all three books, to be explored further in *The Book of Dust*.

The cosmic dilemma: Dust is leaving all the known worlds, draining out through windows (cut by the subtle knife) and through man-induced events with unforeseen consequences.

Experimental Theology • In Lyra's world, Jordan College is preeminent in the study of this field, known as physics in Will's world. The purpose of the study in Lyra's world is to understand what constitutes nature's smallest components down to the atomic level.

Intercision • The process by which a child is separated from its dæmon, these experiments are being carried out in Bolvangar under the supervision of Mrs. Coulter.

Oblation Board • Also called the General Oblation Board, it was established by Mrs. Coulter who is investigating the attraction of Dust to adults. The board's experiments, carried out at Bolvangar, involve a process called intercision: severing the invisible connection between a person and his dæmon. By doing so, Mrs. Coulter hopes to gain a deeper understanding of what Dust is, under the guise of "helping" children, who are naive to her persuasive charms. ("Oblation" means making an offering, and it has religious connotations.)

COMMENTS ABOUT *THE GOLDEN COMPASS*

An Amazon.com editorial review • "In *The Golden Compass,* Philip Pullman has written a masterpiece that transcends genre. It is a children's book that will appeal to adults, a fantasy novel that will charm even the most hardened realist. Best of all, the author doesn't speak down to his audience, nor does he pull his punches; there is genuine terror in this book, and heartbreak, betrayal, and loss. There is also love, loyalty, and an abiding morality that infuses the story but never overwhelms it. This is one of those rare novels that one wishes would never end."

Chris Weitz, director of *The Golden Compass,* in an interview from www.BridgetotheStars.net • "I had heard from friends of mine about a fantastic and life-changing British fantasy series that was 'written for children but really for adults.' I was absolutely stunned by the imagination, daring, and intelligence of the book. . . . To me, it was and is one of the great works of imagination of the twentieth century. I had grown up on Tolkien but this, to be honest, left him in the dust as far as ambition and philosophical depth."

SFReviews.net • "Pullman combines the traditional sense of wonder that one expects to find in epic adventure stories with an atmosphere of elegant eeriness and dreamlike portent. The effect is almost intoxicating. Few fantasists this side of Clark Ashton Smith or A. Merritt have managed to evoke it so effectively. Memorable characters, settings, and scenes simply spill from this story like fruit from the fabled horn of plenty."

Terry Brooks, fantasy author • "*The Golden Compass* is one of the best fantasy/adventure stories that I have read in years. This is a book no one should miss."

Washington Post • "Arguably the best juvenile fantasy novel of the past twenty years. . . . If *[The Subtle Knife]* is as good as *The Golden Compass,* we'll be two-thirds of the way to the completion of a modern fantasy classic."

New Statesman • "Once in a lifetime a children's author emerges who is so extraordinary that the imagination of generations is altered. Lewis Carroll, E. Nesbit, C. S. Lewis, and Tolkien were all of this cast. So, too, is Philip Pullman, whose Dark Materials trilogy will be devoured by anyone between eight and eighty. The most ambitious work since *The Lord of the Rings,* it is as intellectually thrilling as it is magnificently written."

Horn Book Magazine • "The characters of Lord Asriel, Mrs. Coulter, and Iorek Byrnison and the cold and beautiful northern setting are captivating; the constantly twisting plot and escalating suspense are riveting; and Lyra and Pantalaimon are among the gutsiest and wiliest of adventurers. Touching, exciting, and mysterious by turns, this is a splendid work."

One of 150 limited-edition jigsaw puzzles made of
wood; manufactured for the National Theatre

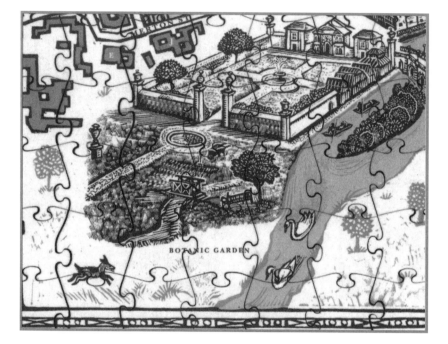

A close-up of the Botanic Garden in a
wooden puzzle made by Longstaff Workshops

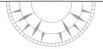

THE SUBTLE KNIFE

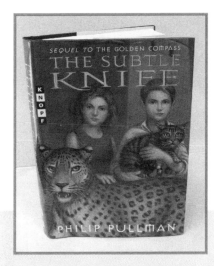

Published in 1997
by Alfred A. Knopf

Cover art by Eric Rohmann

Available in hardback, trade paperback, paperback, and unabridged audiobook on compact disc

Jacket copy: "The universe has broken wide, and Lyra's friend lies dead. Desperate for answers and set on revenge, Lyra bursts into a new world in pursuit of his killer. Instead, she finds Will, just twelve years old and already a murderer himself. He's on a quest as fierce as Lyra's, and together they strike out into this sunlit otherworld.

"But Cittàgazze is a strange and haunted place. Soul-eating Spectres stalk its streets while, high above, the wing beats of distant angels sound against the sky. And in the mysterious Torre degli Angeli lurks Cittàgazze's deadly secret—an object of extraordinary and devastating power.

"On this journey marked by danger, Will and Lyra forge ahead. But with every step and each new horror, they move closer to the greatest threat of all—and the shattering truth of their own destiny."

The cover art by Eric Rohmann is a portrait of Lyra and Will with their dæmons. Lyra has her hand on the back of a big cat, a leopard; Will is holding an oversized cat, who will later be given the name Kirjava by a witch, Serafina Pekkala. On the back cover, we see a cityscape against the night sky.

———⊰◈⊱———

Leaving the confines of her own world behind, Lyra finds herself in our world; specifically, in Oxford, England. Her guide is a young boy her age named Will Parry, who has his own destiny to fulfill, in addition to a shared destiny with Lyra of which he is unaware. As Will flees from men pursuing him for reasons unknown, he slips into another world where he finds Lyra in Cittàgazze, a city populated by feral children, since there are no adults to keep them in check. Invisible (to children) spectres haunt the city, feeding on the souls of adults, leaving them alive but listless. There is no there there.

Will is in search of his father, John Parry, an Arctic explorer who vanished without a trace. Lyra, using the alethiometer, is guided to Dr. Mary Malone, who has discovered, and is studying, "Shadows," her term for Dust.

As forces gather to assist Lord Asriel on his ambitious plan to assault Heaven, to overthrow its Kingdom in favor of establishing a Republic of Heaven on Earth, Will discovers his destiny: It is to inherit from Giacomo Paradisi a weapon of extraordinary power, the subtle knife, a knife so sharp that it is capable of dividing atomic particles, enabling Will to cut windows into other worlds.

The knife is the weapon that can destroy the Authority, the false God, who holds sway over the heavenly hosts through his key lieutenant, Metatron, who is poised to seize power himself.

Forces gather: Allies of Lord Asriel head north to join him in his impending battle, but one key figure is missing—Lyra—as Will discovers to his horror. After a battle with cliff-ghasts, he can't find her; he finds only her rucksack with its treasured alethiometer inside.

KEY CHARACTERS, PLACES, AND THINGS

CHARACTERS

Angelica • A young girl who lives in Cittàgazze. Her older brother is Tullio, whose untimely demise she blames on Lyra and Will. This results in a hunt for them led by her.

Angels • Created from Dust, these beings are essentially ethereal and somewhat conform to our physical vision of them. Key angels include Metatron (the Regent of Heaven), Baruch (Metatron's brother), Balthamos, and Xaphania, all of whom play key roles in His Dark Materials. The first angel is the Authority, who passes himself off as the Creator, successfully conning the other angels with that contemptible lie. Angels are not immortal—they can be killed.

Bearer • The name given to him who wields the subtle knife.

Imperial Guard of Muscovy • The well-trained, well-equipped army that serves the Magisterium. It is justifiably feared because of its formidable military training.

Malone, Dr. Mary • A former nun, she's studying Shadow-particles at an Oxford College in Will's world. Later, her involvement with a race of wheeled, highly intelligent creatures (the Mulefa) proves instrumental in her constructing an amber spyglass with which she can see Dust. Her role in helping Will and, particularly, Lyra is pivotal. Her dæmon is an Alpine chough, a fearless bird from the crow family that's known for its friendly nature.

Paradisi, Giacomo • Prior to Will becoming the wielder of the subtle knife, this man was its owner/bearer. He showed Will how to use the knife.

Parry, John • Will's father. A major in the Royal Marines, he's a central figure who is largely offstage in His Dark Materials. He is associated with the Nuniatak dig sponsored by the Institute of Archaeology at Oxford University (Will's world), the Yenesei Pakhtar tribe, Jordan College, a witch named Juta Kamainen, and Lord Asriel. He goes unaccompanied to the north to investigate a rip in the sky (the Aurora Borealis) revealing another world, which he accidentally enters through a window in his own world. Once he journeys into the other world, he sees his dæmon, named Sayan Kotor. He later assumes the name Stanislaus Grumman.

Parry, Will • The son of John Parry, Will is, like Lyra, a central figure in His Dark Materials. His destiny is inextricably linked to Lyra's, and together they take on the world or, more precisely, worlds.

Payne, Dr. Oliver • A colleague of Dr. Mary Malone in Will's world; together they work to investigate the Shadow-particles—Dust.

Spectres • These vampire-like creatures predominantly haunt the "City of the Magpies." They steal the souls from adults, leaving them incapable of doing anything, but do not target children, who are then called "Spectre orphans" because their parents have been "killed."

PLACES

The Bridge • More commonly known as the Bridge to the Stars, this is created by Lord Asriel, though with unintended, and unforeseen, results of staggering significance.

Cittàgazze • Also known as the City of Magpies because its residents can no longer engage in regular trade. Their ranks have been considerably thinned by the presence of soul-eating Spectres, so they must steal from other worlds. The inhabitants in this city are mostly young, semiferal children. Modeled, according to Pullman, after the city of Venice, Cittàgazze is notable for being where the subtle knife was created, at the Tower of the Angels by the Philosophers' Guild.

Fortress • The stronghold of Lord Asriel, it's constructed on a mountain range with tall battlements made of basalt. Its highest point is the Adamant Tower, where he holds meetings with his High Commanders. Like its architect, Lord Asriel, the Fortress is formidable, imposing, unyielding, and not easily conquered.

THINGS

Æsahættr • Another name for the subtle knife, it means "god destroyer."

Philosophers' Guild • A group of learned men who live in the Torre degli Angeli in Cittàgazze; they invent the subtle knife but know not of its consequences when used. (This can be seen as a metaphor for the misuse of power, which is the result of power untempered by attendant knowledge, a principal concern of Pullman's.)

Subtle Knife • This eight-inch long knife is so sharp that it can cut any known substance. It can be wielded by only one person at a time. Its blade is so fine that it can cut through the fabric of time, opening windows into parallel dimensions, other worlds.

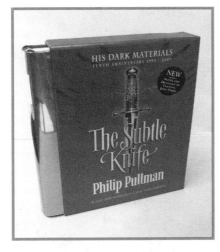

The limited edition of The Subtle Knife, published in the U.K.

COMMENTS ABOUT *THE SUBTLE KNIFE*

Detroit Free Press • "Pullman is a remarkable writer and his trilogy seems destined to become a classic."

New York Times Book Review • "Put Philip Pullman on the shelf with Ursula K. Le Guin, Susan Cooper, Lloyd Alexander. . . . The story gallops with ferocious momentum [and] Pullman is devilishly inventive."

American Bookseller • "A great, sad, lovely book that puzzles over the very transient natures of morality, truth, and duty, *The Subtle Knife* is exquisitely crafted, cover to cover."

Kerry Fried for Amazon.com • "Throughout, Pullman is in absolute control of his several worlds, his plot and pace equal to his inspiration. Any number of astonishing scenes—small- and large-scale—will have readers on edge, and many are cause for tears. . . . It is Philip Pullman's gift to turn what quotidian minds would term the impossible into a reality that is both heartbreaking and beautiful."

Writer Michael Chabon in the *New York Review of Books* • "*The Subtle Knife,* with its shifting points of view and its frequent presentation of adult perspectives on Lyra and Will, has much more the flavor of a thriller. It is unflaggingly inventive, chilling and persuasive, has a number of gripping action sequences, and ends with a thrilling zeppelin battle in the Himalayas."

73

The limited edition of The Amber Spyglass *(U.K. edition)*

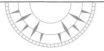

THE AMBER SPYGLASS

*Published in 2000
by Alfred A. Knopf*

Cover art by Eric Rohmann

*Available in hardback, trade
paperback, paperback, and
unabridged audiobook on
compact disc*

Jacket copy. "Lyra and Will . . . are in unspeakable danger.
With help from Iorek Byrnison the armored bear and two
tiny Gallivespian spies, they must journey to a dank and
gray-lit world where no living soul has ever gone.

"All the while, Dr. Mary Malone builds a magnificent
amber spyglass. An assassin hunts her down. And Lord
Asriel, with troops of shining angels, fights his mighty rebel-
lion, a battle of strange allies—and shocking sacrifice.

"As war rages and Dust drains from the sky, the fate of the
living—and the dead—finally comes to depend on two children and the simple truth of one simple story."

A striking departure from his cover art for the first and second books, this third book has a paper-on-board cover. On the front cover, two central figures—Lyra and Will—are surrounded by an ocean of nebulous souls, as two Gallivespians on their dragonfly steeds circle above them. The back cover shows a sea of disenchanted souls, condemned to live in the land of the dead.

The longest and most complex of the three books, *The Amber Spyglass* is a battleground of confrontations. The Church is hell-bent on killing Lyra, Lord Asriel's forces confront the Church's, Lyra and Will must fight and win over the Harpies that guard the land of the dead, and Metatron and his heavenly host make an assault against Lord Asriel's stronghold. At stake: not only Lyra's world but Will's world, and the countless parallel universes as well. Meanwhile, Dust is continuing to escape and it's up to Will wielding the subtle knife to stem its flow.

⸻

The Amber Spyglass won the prize in 2001 not only for the prestigious Whitbread Children's Book of the Year but the Whitbread Book of the Year Award, sponsored by the Whitbread Breweries company.

KEY CHARACTERS, PLACES, AND THINGS

CHARACTERS

Ama • A young girl who brings food to Mrs. Coulter at her hideout in the Himalayas. Ama's dæmon is named Kulang, which is the name of a Himalayan mountain that stands 4822 feet tall.

Balthamos (angelic being) • This angel and another named Baruch are allies of Will. Both support the efforts of a rebel angel named Xaphania. Balthamos and Baruch clearly love each other, in the best sense of the word; they are soul mates.

Baruch (angelic being) • Formerly a man, his brother was Enoch, who is now known as Metatron, the Regent of Heaven. Like other mortals, Baruch was destined to go to the world of the dead but was spared that fate by an angel named Balthamos who transforms Baruch into an angel.

Boatman (immortal being) • He is the ferryman who transports ghosts to the land of the dead in his small watercraft. His old and crippled appearance belies his immortality. Like Charon (from Greek mythology), he carries a heavy burden but dutifully fulfills his task: Countless millions have, at his hands, made their final trip; in this case, to a bleak landscape, colorless and joyless, where all hope is lost—a place of eternal limbo.

Death • Inspired by the Grim Reaper, this spectral entity is an integral part of oneself but cannot be seen until the end of one's life when it accompanies the recently departed on a journey to the land of the dead.

Dragonflies • Bred by the Gallivespians to be ridden, and outfitted with riding harnesses, these are larger in size than those in Will's world.

Father Gomez • A member of the Consistorial Court of Discipline, he is invested with a special task that, if successful, will change the future of Lyra's world and all the other worlds, as well. His dæmon is a large beetle, which is rather appropriate, as a beetle is hardy and can survive under adverse conditions; it's also a natural predator of other insects.

Gallivespians • No more than a few inches in height, this short-lived, humanoid race is formidable because of the poison in the spurs of their heels, which is capable of killing a grown man. They use specially bred dragonflies for flying steeds.

Ghost • Upon death, a human becomes a ghost, which then must find its way to the land of the dead, established by the Authority. Wispy in substance, ghosts cannot speak above a whisper; they are in every way a mere shadow of their former selves.

Harpies • Appointed by the Authority to watch over the ghosts in the land of the dead, these winged, malevolent creatures have one mission: to continually remind each ghost of its every mistake committed during its lifetime. Their constant assault makes it impossible for the ghosts to have even a moment to themselves. Theirs is a life of eternal torment, on which the harpies feed psychically. (A Greek myth was Pullman's inspiration for these creatures.)

Kirjava • The name given by Serafina Pekkala to Will's dæmon, a large cat with lustrous fur.

Metatron • The central figure in *The Amber Spyglass,* he is the de facto ruler of the Kingdom of Heaven. Formerly a man with mortal failings, Metatron is a powerful angel who, in many ways, is a counterpart to Lord Asriel: Both are extraordinary, powerful, and strong-willed, though not strong enough to resist the allure of Mrs. Coulter, a fatal flaw that proves to be both their downfalls.

Mulefa • From another world, this species befriends Dr. Mary Malone in her search for Dust. Respectful of nature, with an innate ability to see

Dust, the members of this species are approximately the size of deer, with unusual, adaptive legs: a front leg, two side-by-side legs, and a rear leg, each clawed, giving them the ability to use seedpods as wheels. They propel themselves with their middle legs.

Roke, Lord • One of the High Commanders under Lord Asriel, he is the leader of the Gallivespians. He oversees the spying operations through his subordinates, Chevalier Tialys and the Lady Salmakia; they communicate by way of a curious device called the lodestone resonator.

Salmakia, Lady • She is a Gallivespian spy who works for Lord Roke. Her mission is to infiltrate the Society of the Work of the Holy Spirit and report back to him.

Tialys, Chevalier • A Gallivespian spy for Lord Roke, he uses a lodestone resonator to file reports. Tialys's mission is to spy on the Consistorial Court of Discipline.

Tualapi • These large birds terrorize the Mulefa and take their precious seedpods.

Xaphania • A rebel female angel who leads an angelic host, she is one of Lord Asriel's High Commanders (the others include Lord Roke and Madame Oxentiel, both Gallivespians, and King Ogunwe of Africa). It is Xaphania who is credited for discovering the truth about the Authority: Created out of Dust, he is the first entity formed as an angel who convinces fellow angels that he is the supreme being in existence. Xaphania, a fallen angel, has much in common with Milton's Satan as depicted in *Paradise Lost*.

PLACES

Abyss • A bottomless pit created when a bomb was detonated, through which Dust is escaping.

Adamant Tower • The highest vantage point of Lord Asriel's stronghold, in his basalt fortress.

Botanic Gardens • Found in both Lyra and Will's worlds, this is a place where both meet on an ongoing basis, albeit under unusual circumstances.

THINGS

Amber Spyglass • Dr. Mary Malone constructs this telescope using the sap from the seedpod trees favored by the Mulefa. With it, she can see Dust, which is escaping at record rates.

Gyropter • An aircraft used by Lord Asriel's troops. It's similar to a helicopter.

Intention Craft • A mechanical marvel with six legs and a cockpit, it is flown by one's intentions, hence its name. It is highly maneuverable and heavily armed (similar to a Cobra gunship).

Laquer • This distilled tree sap, produced by the Mulefa, is what Dr. Mary Malone uses to construct the lenses of her singular amber spyglass, which allows her to see Dust.

Land of the Dead • The ghostly dead live in eternal limbo in a featureless, dimly lit place, a barren terrain.

Lodestone Resonator • A communications device used by the Gallivespians. Not mechanical or electrical in nature, its principal feature is that it resonates using a bow manipulated by a small stone pencil. This is the primary means that Chevalier Tialys uses to keep in touch with Lord Roke.

Quantum Entanglement Bomb • A highly discriminate, high-tech weapon that detonates when nearing its intended victim, a target identified through DNA analysis.

Seedpods • The giant, round seeds are ridden by the Mulefa. It is a sign of adulthood when a Mulefa gets its first pod.

79

COMMENTS ABOUT *THE AMBER SPYGLASS*

Sunday Journal • "A breathtaking and stunning grand finale. . . . Its tense drama combines with stark, powerfully emotional scenes to weave a superbly imaginative achievement in speculative fiction."

VOYA **(Voice of Youth Advocates)** • "The writing is flawless, the imaginative vision is breathtaking, and the conclusion is heartbreaking but fitting and proper. At the close of this masterpiece, the reader can only marvel at Pullman's genius, alternately weeping and rejoicing for one's humanity. All who read it will come away enriched, enlightened, and aching for a dæmon of one's own."

David Pickering for Amazon.co.uk • "The pace of the book is compelling, the writing powerful. Pullman's plotting is intricate and cunning, surprising the reader again and again. Perhaps what is most striking of all, however, is the depth of the characterisation. Lord Asriel, Mrs. Coulter, Iorek Byrnison the king of the armoured bears, a host of minor characters, most of all Will and Lyra themselves: the book is a library of beautifully drawn, remarkably convincing characters walking in worlds of marvels.

"In this volume the cosmic dimensions of the story become more prominent, as a great conflict across many universes comes to a head—how well the narrative sustains such immensely weighty resonances is a question critics may well disagree on. The author's beliefs also come more into the open, and with them a polemic anti-religious theme that will please some readers and alienate others.

"Philip Pullman's writing commands immense respect; more than that, it is raising the profile of the best children's books among adults, as demanding critics of all ages fall in love with this remarkable trilogy."

Publishers Weekly • "In concluding the spellbinding His Dark Materials trilogy, Pullman produces what may well be the most controversial children's book of recent years. . . . Along the way, Pullman riffs on the elemental chords of classical myth and fairy tale. While some sections seem rushed and the prose is not always as brightly polished as fans might expect, Pullman's exuberant work stays rigorously true to its own internal structure. Stirring and highly provocative."

Stephanie Merritt for the *Observer* • "This is a gripping, erudite and vivid novel, full of magic—parallel worlds, talking armoured bears and demons, the animal incarnations of the soul—but solidly anchored in real emotions. To describe it as 'fantasy' would be as reductive as to label it 'children's fiction.'"

Formally titled **Portrait of Cecilia Gallerani,** *it's better known as* **Lady with an Ermine.** *Painted by Leonardo da Vinci, the portrait was cited by Philip Pullman as being very nearly a portrait of Lyra and Pan.*

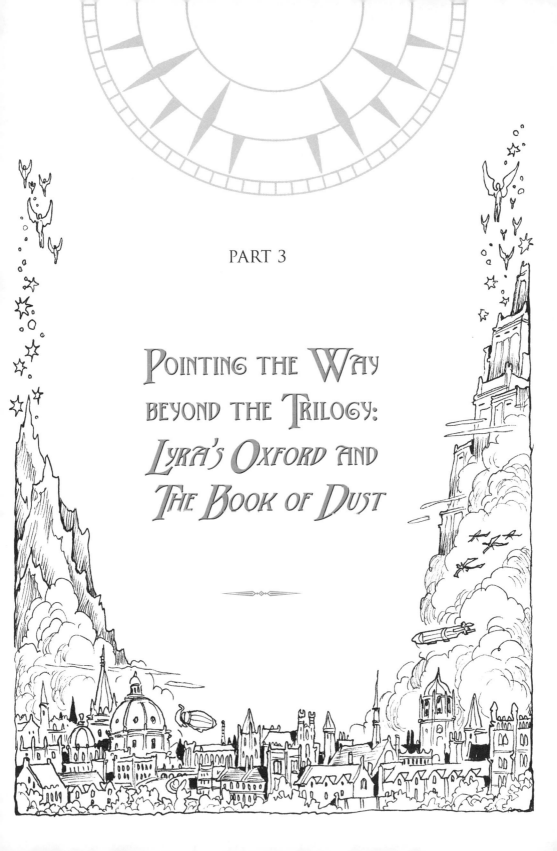

PART 3

POINTING THE WAY BEYOND THE TRILOGY: *LYRA'S OXFORD* AND *THE BOOK OF DUST*

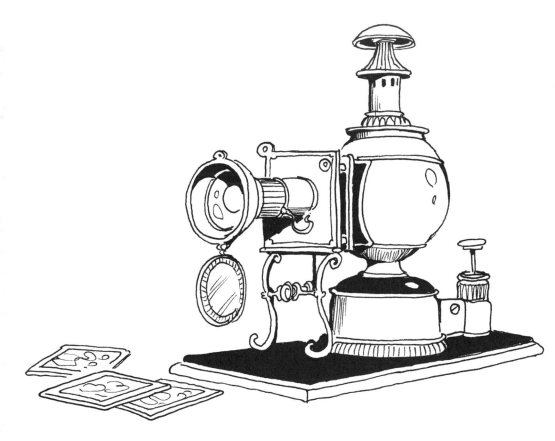

Projecting Lantern

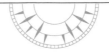

LYRA'S OXFORD

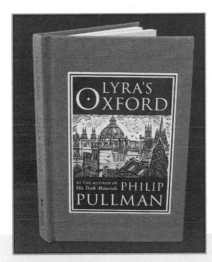

*Published in 2000
by Alfred A. Knopf*

A David Fickling Book

*Trade hardback, forty-nine
numbered pages plus five
pages of supplementary material. Includes a "Globetrotter"
map of the Polar Regions and
a bound-in map of Lyra's
Oxford. Also available as an
unabridged audiobook.*

The elegantly packaged, unabridged audiobook adaptation is designed as a three-panel insert in a paper slipcase; the
first panel is an envelope that holds a fold-out map of Lyra's
Oxford, with liner notes reproducing the supplementary
material. The audio version lacks the "Globetrotter: Polar
Regions Arctic map." Narrated by Philip Pullman, this
production's cast includes: Douglas Blackwell as Sebastian
Makepeace and Mr. Shuter, Daniel Flynn as Dr. Polstead,
Garrick Hagon as Ms. Greenwood's Dæmon, Anton Lesser
as Ragi, Nicolette McKenzie as Ms. Greenwood, Richard
Pearce as Pantalaimon, Liza Ross as Ruth, and Jo Wyatt as
Lyra.

Pullman's readers, whose appetites had been whetted for *The Book of Dust,* found themselves pleasantly surprised when, in November 2003, David Fickling Books published a small hardback book containing an episode from Lyra's life, set two years after the end of *The Amber Spyglass.* The cover to *Lyra's Oxford* sports an iconic illustration by John Lawrence, renowned for his woodcuts. In the illustration (a view of Oxford as seen by Lyra, who frequents its rooftops) we see the Radcliffe Camera (among other landmarks) and a flock of starlings.

In an interview for the *Guardian Unlimited* (April 6, 2003), publisher David Fickling explains the genesis of the book:

> I asked Philip if he could do some bits and pieces around the idea of a map and this book grew out of it. He always told me he couldn't write short stories, but it isn't true. Lyra is there right from the beginning with her dæmon Pantalaimon and there will even be a postcard from this parallel Oxford.

Pullman elaborates, "The book will consist of much more than just the story. We wanted to create an object that was both intriguing and beautiful, and—like the story—was both self-contained and full of references elsewhere."

A bridge to Pullman's *The Book of Dust,* this elegantly designed book is a masterful job of book production. Published in hardback, it has no dust jacket; instead, its red cloth cover bears an adhesive woodblock illustration (on the front) and an outlined map of England. (Among Pullman's books, it's his favorite in terms of design.)

The quotation that sets the stage for the story that follows is by Oscar Baedecker, the purported author of *The Coasts of Bohemia.* Like everything else in this book, his quote straddles fact and fiction. There is a book with that title, but its real-world author is Derek Sayer. Oscar Baedecker's last

Unabridged recording of **Lyra's Oxford**

name has its own story. According to the *Travel Industry Dictionary,* "Baedecker" was: "Originally a series of guidebooks published in

Germany in the late nineteenth century, now used generically or metaphorically for guides in general." Verlag Karl Baedeker founded the German book publishing company in 1827 that bears his name (www.baedeker.com).

What's interesting to me is that in the prefatory quotation for *Lyra's Oxford,* Baedecker speaks of Oxford as "where the real and the unreal jostle in the streets . . . where the river mists have a solvent and vivifying effect on the stone of the ancient buildings . . . where windows open into other worlds . . ." The fictional Baedecker, talking about the duality of Oxford—its reality and air of unreality—parallels closely what Pullman wrote in a *Guardian* essay (July 27, 2002):

> I put it down to the mists from the river, which have a solvent effect on reality. A city where South Parade is in the north and North Parade is in the south, where Paradise is lost under a car park, where the Magdalen gargoyles climb down at night and fight with those from New College, is a place where, as I began by saying, likelihood evaporates.

We see this melding of fact and fiction, reality and unreality, in the supplementary materials that comprise this small book. For instance, in an advertisement for "Books on travel, archaeology, and related subject," its authors include Marisa Coulter (Mrs. Coulter, Lyra's mother) as the author of *The Bronze Clocks of Benin,* and Nicholas Outram (Pullman's middle names) as the author of *Some Curious Anomalies in the Mathematics of Palladio's Quattro Libri.* Furthermore, Professor P. Trelawney is the author of *Fraud: An Exposure of a Scientific Imposture;* he's a Palmerian Professor at Jordan College who's present in the Retiring Room when Lord Asriel presents his case for more funding to the Jordan scholars.

More references, direct and indirect, abound in the supplementary materials:

A postcard (sent by Mary Malone) shows four scenes of Oxford, including a street with hornbeam trees, and a bench in the Botanic Gardens where Lyra and Will sat;

An annotated Globetrotter map of the "Polar Regions: Arctic," donated by Lord Asriel to the Jordan College Library;

References to catalogues containing camping equipment, cold-weather clothing, navigational equipment (including compasses), surveying equipment (again, compasses), and materials used by artists and draughtsmen. (All allude to the ill-fated Grumman expedition.)

The deliberately ambiguous introduction to the book states that "This book contains a story and several other things. The other things might be connected with the story, or they might not; they might be connected to stories that haven't appeared yet. It's not easy to tell." It's a classic Pullman observation, variations of which he's written in essays for the *Guardian* newspaper, in which he's talked about matters being either "this" or "that." In other words, open-ended, open to interpretation, and deliberately ambiguous—like life itself, an eternal mystery.

Set two years after *The Amber Spyglass*, the short story begins with Lyra and Pan (now settled as a pine marten) on the roof of the Lodge Tower where they observe a large flock of starlings relentlessly attacking a witch's dæmon-bird, "a dark bird about the size of a thrush" that has come in search of Lyra.

To say anything more would be to spoil for you the delight of reading the story yourself, so I'll keep mum.

Pantalaimon as a pine marten

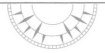

THE BOOK OF DUST

ike most authors, Pullman is reluctant to discuss works in progress, so what little we know about *The Book of Dust* comes from snippets of interviews he's given over the years.

Quoted in the column "Letters from London" (*Publishers Weekly,* March 5, 2001), Pullman explains:

> *The Book of Dust* will not be a simple reference book—far from it. I want to go into the background of Lyra's world, and the creation myth that underpins the whole trilogy, and to say something about some of the other characters, and about the alethiometer and the history of the subtle knife, and so on. Furthermore I want it to be richly illustrated. It'll be story-driven, not reference-driven, and I'll need to brood over it in silence before I find the right form for it.

More details were forthcoming from a form letter that Pullman sent out to curious readers who wrote to him, hoping for a reply. "Thank you for writing to me. I wish I could reply to every letter personally, but it would be impossible to do that *and* write more books."

In the letter, Pullman provides more details about what we can expect in *The Book of Dust*:

> For those who want to know more about His Dark Materials: the story of Will and Lyra is at an end, but I know that a lot of readers would like to see more of the world of the story, and read not only about those two characters, but about others as well, and about the background; and some people are wondering about the religious aspects of the story,

too. I have a lot to say about all of those things, and I want to put together a sort of companion volume that will answer some of those questions and explain more about the worlds in which the story takes place. That book will be called *The Book of Dust.* . . . Then there are some other characters whose stories I want to find out more about, such as Lee Scoresby the Texas aeronaut, and Serafina Pekkala the witch. I want to tell the story of how Lee first met Iorek Byrnison, and how Serafina Pekkala fell in love with the Gyptian Farder Coram when he was a young man. There are lots of stories to tell!

Gyropters

PART 4

Dæmon Driven: Encompassing Philip Pullman

Just as Pullman's autobiographical essay
("I have a feeling all this belongs to me")
sheds light on him, this section talks more
about Pullman as an artist, shows Pullman's
Oxford, and gives a few select comments
by him pulled from various interviews,
profiles, and essays by and about him.

THE GOLDEN COMPASS

Close-up of the teaser poster (27 x 40 inches) of The Golden Compass *movie, available for $19.95 from shop.newline.com*

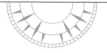

DRAWING ON DESIGN:
PULLMAN AS ARTIST

hen David Fickling of Scholastic UK suggested to Philip Pullman that His Dark Materials be illustrated, Pullman offered his services. But you're not an illustrator, Fickling protested. I could be, replied Pullman.

As Pullman explained on his website, he then auditioned for the job by drawing two illustrations for *The Golden Compass* (chapter 10, "The Consul and the Bear"; chapter 17, "The Witches").

Pullman submitted the samples and Fickling "gave me my first job as a professional illustrator," said Pullman.

Though early editions of His Dark Materials lack the illustrations, the more recent editions feature Pullman's art, little miniature masterpieces that measure 2.6 inches square. Drawn on white Bristol board, the evocative drawings encapsulate each of the books' chapters. Consider chapter 1 of *The Golden Compass,* "The Decanter of Tokay," with its illustration of a decanter of Tokay on its side, its contents spilled and pooling; nearby, Pan in his moth-shape is investigating the spill. Though miniature-sized when printed in the book, the art is stark and stands out.

Chapter 2, "The Idea of North," with its illustration of a movie projector, is a reference to the lantern set up to project the images Lord Asriel took in the polar regions, where he saw a city in the sky— another world, observable in the northern lights, the Aurora Borealis.

Philip Pullman

Decanter of Tokay

Though Fickling was understandably surprised to discover that the writer Philip Pullman also had artistic talent, it would not have surprised those who knew Pullman when he was growing up. Early on, he showed a great interest in art; so much so, in fact, that he wished he had majored in art and not literature in college.

Pullman, a self-taught artist, realized that good illustration serves the storyteller; text, when paired with appropriate drawings, enriches the storytelling experience for the reader—something Pullman recognized at a young age, when he saw the power of the comic book format to tell stories visually.

Not surprisingly, Pullman has a good eye for art. When Knopf selected a cover artist for its edition of *The Golden Compass,* they turned to Eric Rohmann, who rendered an evocative illustration of Lyra and Pan on Iorek's back. Lyra's expression is innocent, Iorek's inscrutable. In that picture, we see a world of possibilities—infinite possibilities, which Pullman wrote about in an essay for the *Horn Book Magazine* (July/August 2003):

> Mr. Rohmann has done something miraculous with Lyra's face. The story depicts her poised between childhood and adulthood, on the very cusp of adolescence—and poised between several other things as well. . . . Mr. Rohmann's picture shows her exactly balanced between a past and a future, between safety and danger, between one world and another, between a thousand possibilities in one direction and millions of possibilities in another. It's a face full of dreams and full of wonder. It is Lyra as she truly is, better than I could ever have hoped to see her pictured.

Rohmann would go on to draw two more covers, for *The Subtle Knife* and *The Amber Spyglass,* with remarkable results: For *The Subtle Knife,* we see Lyra and Will with their respective dæmons; for *The Amber Spyglass,* we see Lyra and Will encircled by a sea of dead spirits as two Gallivespians on their winged mounts approach them. (To my mind, Rohmann's art for *The Golden Compass* remains the most enchanting.)

As good as Rohmann's art is, I prefer Pullman's because he is, after all, the author whose imagination brought everything in Lyra's world to life. The miniatures printed as chapter head illustrations for all three books make one wish for larger, more detailed art, and perhaps some in color, as well. Even so, what we have—a body of work, dozens of pieces—goes a long way toward showing us another facet of Pullman's imagination.

On Pullman's website, the illustrations for *The Golden Compass* and *The Subtle Knife* are published with explanatory texts. For the illustration in the first chapter of *The Golden Compass,* we see "The Decanter of Tokay . . . spilled, but not broken as it is in the text. A broken decanter could be anything; here at least we can still see what it is. And Pantalaimon in his moth-shape is coming to investigate."

Of all the drawings, surely the most evocative is the tiny portrait of Lyra, for chapter 23, "The Bridge to the Stars." It's the final chapter of *The Golden Compass.* Pullman notes that it was "the hardest drawing of all." She is looking up at the city in the sky and, symbolically, Pullman draws no borders around the picture because he deliberately wants to suggest that "The boundaries are all dissolved." Lyra will soon put her familiar world behind her to discover new ones.

As for further illustrations of Lyra's world by Pullman, we will have to wait and see. *Lyra's Oxford* had no art by Pullman, though he clearly could have rendered some small illustrations or devices. And it's too early to speculate on what Pullman may do in terms of illustrations for *The Book of Dust,* but it is surely a book that demands proper illustration!

*Philip Pullman's website, featuring reproductions
and explanations of his art for His Dark Materials*

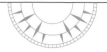

SUNDRY COMMENTS
BY PHILIP PULLMAN

ON HIS DARK MATERIALS: "I thought it would be hard to find an audience for this story, and I've been astonished and delighted by the reception it's had all over the world. I don't want to say very much about it here, because I'd like it to speak for itself." (Pullman's website)

ON THE STORYTELLER'S RESPONSIBILITY: "I've been telling stories for many years now, and in the course of that experience I've come to see a few things more clearly than I used to. I take it that art, literature, children's literature, does not exist in a special realm apart from society. I take it that storytellers are inextricably part of the whole world, and that one way of thinking about the relationship between art and society is to approach it by considering the responsibilities that follow from this." ("Voluntary service," *Guardian,* Dec. 28, 2002)

ON DUST: "I've taken a leap beyond anything the science justifies—I don't think any scientist has ever come up with the idea that dark matter is conscious! Dust is all the wisdom and consciousness of the world, which has somehow become externalised. You can even say it's an atheist's God. But it's a mutually dependent thing: to make sure Dust doesn't vanish we have to contribute to wisdom as well as leech from it." (Pullman quoted by Celia Dodd in "Debate: Human Nature: Universally Acknowledged," *Times Online,* May 8, 2004)

ON FANTASY FICTION: "It is not that I don't like fantasy, I don't like what it does. Fantasy, and fiction in general, is failing to do what it might be doing. It has unlimited potential to explore all sorts of metaphysical and moral questions, but it is not . . . my quarrel with fantasy writing is that it is such a rich seam to be mined, such a versatile mode, that is not always being used to explore bigger ideas." (Pullman quoted by Angelique Chrisafis in "Pullman lays down moral challenge for writers," *Guardian,* Aug, 12, 2002)

ON JORDAN COLLEGE: "Jordan College occupies the same physical space in Lyra's Oxford (Lyra is the young heroine of my story) as Exeter College occupies in real life, though rather more of it. Exeter was where I was an undergraduate many years ago, and I did not see why I should not make my college the grandest of all. Jordan, where Lyra grows up, has developed in a haphazard, piecemeal way, and for all its wealth some part of it is always about to fall down and is consequently covered in scaffolding; it has an air of jumbled and squalid grandeur." (Pullman, "Dreaming of spires," *Guardian,* July 27, 2002)

ON MYTH: "We all need some sort of myth. Some sort of over-arching narrative to live by. For hundreds of years in the West, this need was fulfilled by the Christian story, but that is now either dead or dying." (Pullman quoted by Robert McCrum in "Dæmon Geezer," *Observer,* Jan. 27, 2002)

ON WORKS IN PROGRESS AND FUTURE WORKS: "After *The Book of Dust,* that will be enough. But my publisher had an intriguing suggestion: after *Lyra's Oxford,* which is a dark-red book, he said, 'Why don't you do a little dark-green book?' So: *The Book of Dust,* then a little dark-green book, and then that's it." (Pullman quoted in an interview with *Books Quarterly,* a publication by the British bookseller Waterstone's, date not known)

ON PULLMAN'S RELIGIOUS VIEWS: "Well, it is not that I hate God, it is just because I don't believe in God, it is just that I think the people who do believe in God and persecute the people who don't believe in God are thoroughly dangerous, that is the way I would put it. People who have got an idea of God that makes them want to persecute other people for not believing their idea of God, they are the dangerous ones, people who say we have got the truth and the truth is in the Bible or the Koran or whatever it is and we know the truth, and we are going to kill everybody who doesn't believe things that we believe, that is a dreadful state of affairs and it is an unfortunate part of human nature that it seems to be attracted to this sort of extreme certainty and arrogance." (In response to a question from Kent Simon, a young reader, during a live interview on BBC Newsround, Jan. 23, 2002, after the announcement that he had won the Whitbread Award)

ON COMIC BOOKS: "Comic books changed my life because I saw for the first time an entirely new way of telling stories. The combination of words and pictures, of effortlessly vivid storytelling, made me want to tell stories more than anything else." (Pullman quoted in an interview on KidsReads.com, Dec. 12, 2001)

ON LYRA AND THE STORYTELLING PROCESS: "Just as Lyra is growing up, accumulating new experiences and seeing the world in a wider and more complex way, so the reader is doing that as well. The structure of the trilogy is mirroring the consciousness of a growing, learning, developing consciousness. The story widens out; we have the perspective of a lot of characters instead of one. . . . You have to give the reader some sense of this large scale and the many strands of narrative in the story. And those many strands also allowed me to vary the pace. From moments of high stress and danger, I could move to another part of the story and have a few pages of quiet and peace." (Pullman in an exclusive interview conducted by Dave Weich of Powells.com, Aug. 21, 2000)

ON THE KINGDOM OF HEAVEN: "The kingdom of heaven promised us certain things: it promised us happiness and a sense of purpose and a sense of having a place in the universe, of having a role and a destiny that were noble and splendid; and so we were connected to things. We were not alienated. But now that, for me anyway, the King is dead, I find that I still need these things that heaven promised, and I'm not willing to live without them. I don't think I will continue to live after I'm dead, so if I am to achieve these things I must try to bring them about—and encourage other people to bring them about—on earth, in a republic in which we are all free and equal—and responsible—citizens." (Pullman interviewed by Huw Spanner in "Heat and Dust," *Third Way,* Feb. 13, 2002)

ON THE ORIGIN OF THE IDEA OF DÆMONS: "When I first saw Lyra in my mind's eye, there was someone or something close by, which I realised was an important part of her. When I wrote the first four words of *Northern Lights* ("Lyra and her dæmon"), the relationship suddenly sprang into focus." (Pullman in an exclusive interview for Scholastic.com)

ON THE MAGIC OF THEATERS: "But when everything is working well, something mysterious happens between an audience and a play that isn't just the sum of the component parts. . . . But something happens, and everything is transformed. We could use a scientific term like emergence

97

for this process, or we could use an older world and call it sorcery; but whatever we call it, there's no point in trying to explain it to those who insist on a functional justification for everything, those who can only see value in an activity if it brings in money from tourists, or helps children with their GCSEs. They'll never understand." (Pullman in "Let's pretend," *Guardian,* Nov. 24, 2004)

ON THEOCRACIES AND READING: "So the trouble with the way theocracies read is that they have a narrow idea of what literature is: They think it only contains one kind of thing, and has only one purpose, which is a narrowly political one. . . . The theocratic cast of mind is always reductive whether it's in power or not." (Pullman in "The war on words," *Guardian,* Nov. 6, 2004)

ON CHILDREN NEEDING THE ARTS: "Children need art and music and literature; they need to go to art galleries and museums and theatres; they need to learn to play musical instruments and to act and to dance. They need these things so much that human rights legislation alone should ensure that they get them." (Pullman, "Theatre—the true key stage," *Guardian,* March 30, 2004)

ON MOTIVATIONS FOR WRITING: "We all write out of our obsessions, conscious or unconscious, and if we try to move too far away from the things that move us most deeply, our work will lack substance and fail to nourish. The activity of storytelling, the sense I have of its importance, is something that's central in my own work, so it's not surprising that it turns up in the things I write." (Pullman interviewed by downhomebooks.com, Oct. 2004)

ON SPIRITUALITY: "I don't use the word spiritual myself, because I don't have a clear sense of what it means. But I think it depends on your view of education: whether you think that the true end and purpose of education is to help children grow up, compete and face the economic challenges of a global environment that we're going to face in the twenty-first century, or whether you think it's to do with helping them see that they are the true heirs and inheritors of the riches—the philosophical, the artistic, the scientific, the literary riches—of the whole world. If you believe in setting children's minds alive and ablaze with excitement and passion or whether it's a matter of filling them with facts and testing on them. It depends on your vision of education—and I know which one I'd go for." (Pullman in an edited version of a Platform at the National

Theatre, in "The Dark Materials debate: life, God, the universe" with the Archbishop of Canterbury, Dr. Rowan Williams, March 17, 2004)

ON THE ALETHIOMETER: "I love the beauty of mechanical devices— orreries, watches, compasses. The alethiometer came out of my interest in the Renaissance, the world described so vividly by Frances Yates in *The Art of Memory* and *The Rosicrucian Enlightenment.* . . . Frances Yeats described the 'memory theatre,' an imaginary construction that you gradually accumulate in your mind; part of rhetorical technique was to memorise every detail of this complex building, and use it to remember the points in a speech by placing them in the form of vivid images. . . . This notion of embodying moral and philosophical ideas in pictures is what lay behind the alethiometer, a device for the divination of truth that works a little like a clock or a compass." (Pullman interviewed by Jennie Renton for textualities.net, 2005)

ON HOW MUCH OF A FACTOR INSPIRATION IS WHEN WRITING: "Less than non-writers think. If you're going to make a living at this business—more importantly, if you're going to write anything that will last—you have to realise that a lot of the time, you're going to be writing without inspiration. The trick is to write just as well without it as with. Of course, you write less readily and fluently without it; but the interesting thing is to look at the private journals and letters of great writers and see how much of the time they just had to do without inspiration. Conrad, for example, groaned at the desperate emptiness of the pages he faced; and yet he managed to cover them. Amateurs think that if they were inspired all the time, they could be professionals. Professionals know that if they relied on inspiration, they'd be amateurs." (From Pullman's website, the FAQs "About the Writing")

ON HIS CONTRIBUTION TO LITERATURE: "My contribution to literature—holy smoke. Well, I'd like my books to live on awhile after I die, and be recommended by one reader to another rather than be part of some critical canon. I'll have the critical approval as well, if it's on offer, but the way I'd most like to be remembered is as a storyteller. Someone said that literature should help us to enjoy life, or to endure it. I'd be happy with either of those valuable aspirations." (Pullman interviewed by Karin Snelson for Amazon.com, no date)

ON WRITING LONG STORIES: "There's nothing like setting out on a long voyage, and beginning a long story is like that. There's a sense of spaciousness, of amplitude. There's a large world in front of you, and you don't know what's in it. You're going to go exploring and you're going to be disconcerted and maybe you're going to be frightened, but you're going to be excited and made happy, too, by what's there. Just this sense of space and size and lots of room." (Pullman interviewed by Dave Weich for Powells.com, Oct. 2003)

ON THE TIME FRAME OF LYRA'S WORLD: "The notion is that it's the present day, because when she comes through into our world, or when Will goes into the world where they meet, it's the present day for Will: It's our 2000. So it's the same date in Lyra's world. I purposely didn't give it a date. The idea is that the worlds split apart at some date in the past and developed differently. Some things have gone ahead, others things have remained static or developed differently, and the technology is different and so on. This comes out of this notion of multiple worlds, which is familiar to readers of popular books of physics and *Scientific American.* (Pullman answering questions from the audience at Lexicon in Oxford, England, Aug. 2000)

ON THE EPIC AS A LITERARY FORM: "Above all, an epic is big. It's about big things—death, courage, honour, war, shame, vengeance. It's about large and public matters—the fate of a nation, the return of a king, the success of an army, the origin of a people. Its protagonists are larger than human beings, and perhaps simpler too: they are not heroes. The preservation of an epic is a matter not of private dilettantism, but of national importance. It is less precious than literature, but more valuable." (Pullman writing on the sixtieth anniversary of the first Penguin classic, the *Odyssey,* published in 1946)

ON HIS CAREER, LOOKING BACK: "If the young boy I used to be could have looked ahead in time and seen the man I am today, writing stories in his shed, would he have been pleased? I wonder. Would that child who loved Batman comics and ghost stories approve of the novels I earn my living with now? I hope so. I hope he's still with me. I'm writing them for him." (Random House's website, "About the Author" for Philip Pullman)

ON WRITING FOR CHILDREN: "In a book for children, you can't put the plot on hold while you cut artistic capers for the amusement of your sophisticated readers because, thank God, your readers are not sophisticated. They've got more important things in mind than your dazzling wordplay. They want to know what happens next." (Pullman quoted by Lili Ladaga in "Philip Pullman weaves spell with His Dark Materials," CNN.com book news, Nov. 10, 2000)

ON LUCK AND HIS CAREER: "Well, I think I have a certain amount of talent; I think that in my time I have worked as hard as I could; but what's beyond doubt is that I have had a very great deal of luck. I know several writers and illustrators of the sort of books that children read who are just as talented as I am, and who have worked just as hard, if not harder, and any of them would richly deserve to stand here today as the recipient of this magnificent award. But I am the one who had the luck. And I'm not yet sixty. I'm still a young man. I have many years left in which to write more stories, and I certainly intend to do exactly that." (Pullman in his lecture at the Swedish Royal Library, delivered on the occasion of his winning the Astrid Lindgren Memorial Award)

ON ADVICE FOR BUDDING WRITERS: "I didn't start with ideas—I never do—I have to start with a picture, a scene, something like that; something intriguing that makes me want to follow it and see what happens. That means that I don't make a plan, because it would prevent more than it allows. There has to be a lot of ignorance in me when I start a story! But that's only MY method. It wouldn't necessarily work for everyone." (In an online discussion titled "Books: The Talk" from *Guardian Unlimited,* in answer to a question posed by a gushing, presumably young, reader whose online name is TheLittleMermaid, posted Jan, 21, 2002)

A DEFENSE ON BEHALF OF JERICHO AND THE OXFORD CANAL, IN THE FACE OF COMMERCIAL ENCROACHMENT: "I love the curious and indeed somewhat gamy character of Jericho and the Oxford canal; it's always seemed to me like a window opening on a quite different world from the academic propriety of its near neighbor, North Oxford. It's a watery, raffish, amiable, trickster-like world of boat-dwellers, horse-dealers and alchemists. The character of this part of Oxford is very ancient, quite unmistakable, entirely unique, and now, alas, in some peril." (Pullman, "Quite unmistakable and entirely unique," *Guardian,* Feb. 23, 2005)

ON FINISHING *THE AMBER SPYGLASS*: "It's taken a long time, and I was reluctant to let it go; I've grown very close to these characters over the past seven years, and it was tempting to think of more scenes and further complications in the story just so I could spend more time with them. But conscience got the better of that—conscience, and a sense that after all this is a story, and it has to obey the story rules, and stop when it comes to an end." (Pullman in a letter from the author on the Random House website)

ON THE CHRISTIAN RESPONSE TO HIS BOOKS: "His Dark Materials seemed to have slipped under their radar whilst Harry Potter, poor thing, took all the flak! . . . A lad from Atlanta wrote to me threatening to sue, although I have yet to hear from his lawyers; some people have openly accused me of 'promoting Satanism,' to which I would argue that they haven't followed the drift of the trilogy at all; finally, the most vicious of my critics in print have been those of the *Catholic Herald,* who seem to me to be nostalgically sharpening their thumbscrews and wishing the Pope would bring back the Inquisition." (Pullman quoted in a Q&A at Balliol College, transcript by Thea Logie, Nov. 6, 2002)

ON HIS EXCITING WRITING LIFE: "Writing. That's what I've been doing. Sitting quietly here at my table, reading, making notes for *The Book of Dust,* writing. And I'm not going to say anything about it except that I expect to be doing exactly that for a long time to come. What a boring life a writer leads! No drama, no adventure or excitement, no tense high-level last-minute dashes to save the world. Nothing thrilling to tell you about. Just sitting at a table and scribbling. Well, it suits me." (Pullman on his website, Aug. 2005 newsletter.)

ON HIS RELIGIOUS BELIEFS: "The question of what term to use is a difficult one. In strict terms I suppose I'm an agnostic because, of course, the circle of the things I do know is vastly smaller than the things I don't know about. Out there in the darkness somewhere, maybe there is a God. But among all the things I do know in this world, I see no evidence of a God whatsoever." (Pullman interviewed by David Frost on "BBC Breakfast with Frost," BBC, Jan. 27, 2002)

ON WHAT TO WRITE: "Write about what YOU want to. Nobody ever said before Harry Potter came along, oh, we must have a book about Harry Potter. You know what you will be able to tell a good story about. So don't let anybody tell you what you should write about. You know best!" (A question posed by fourteen-year-old Alison Thorpe of Cirencester, BBC, 2003)

ON THE IMPORTANCE OF STORIES: "Because they entertain and they teach, they help us both enjoy life and endure it. After nourishment, shelter and companionship, stories are the thing we need most in the world." (Pullman quoted in an interview published by Reading Is Fundamental UK)

ON PULLMAN'S FAVORITE CHARACTER: "I like them all, of course. People are surprised when I say that I like Mrs. Coulter, but what I mean, of course, is that I like writing about her because she's so completely free of any moral constraint. There's nothing she wouldn't do, and that's a great delight for a storyteller because it means your story can be unconstrained, too. I'm not sure I'd like to know her in real life (well, of course I would; she'd be fascinating). Writers have always enjoyed their villains, and so do readers, if they're honest. (Pullman interviewed by Barnes & Noble online: "The Man behind the Magic: An Interview with Philip Pullman")

103

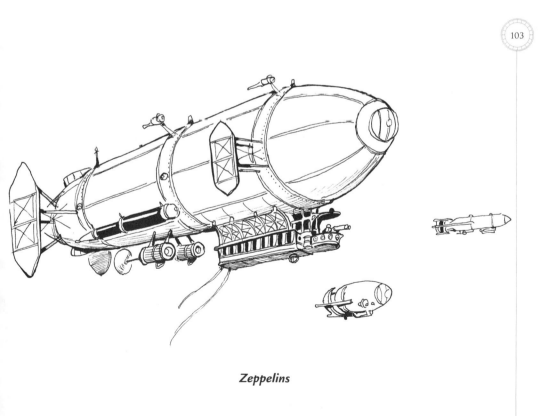

Zeppelins

EMMA RAYNAUD'S GALLERY
OF COLOUR PHOTOGRAMS
OF PULLMAN'S OXFORD

... THAT SWEET CITY WITH HER DREAMING SPIRES.
—Matthew Arnold, "Thrysis"

is Dark Materials begins, and ends, in Oxford, England. It is, as Arnold says, a city with "dreaming spires." It's a city steeped in literary tradition, a scholar's haven (the gown), and heaven for bibliophiles (the town). It's a city where some of the most celebrated books of fantasy have been written: J. R. R. Tolkien's *The Lord of the Rings,* C. S. Lewis's *The Chronicles of Narnia,* and Lewis Carroll's *Alice's Adventures in Wonderland.*

A rooftop view of All Souls College, unique because it's a haven for research, restricted to Fellows only; no students are admitted

The main entrance to the Botanic Garden, where Lyra and Will rendezvous annually in their respective worlds at a specific bench; it is the oldest garden of its kind in the U.K., covering 4.5 acres.

Most recently, Philip Pullman's His Dark Materials draws on the city of Oxford as its principal setting. In an article for *Oxford Today*, Pullman explained: "The first in my trilogy of novels is set partly in an alternate universe, which contains an imaginary Oxford. Imaginary, because the story is a fantasy; but perhaps a great deal of Oxford is imaginary anyway."

A resident of Oxford for thirty-five years, Pullman knows, and loves, this city seemingly tailor-made for an imaginative writer like himself who integrated its geography and prominent landmarks in His Dark Materials, giving the story a texture of reality.

For those fortunate enough to have enjoyed the city's timeless charms as a resident or well-traveled tourist, no guidebook is necessary. But for the rest of us who must be content with armchair travels, several resources come to mind.

Jericho, at the end of the Oxford Canal, is where numerous houseboats are moored. In Lyra's world, it's where the Gyptians dock their boats.

The Ashmolean Museum: The oldest museum in the U.K., it houses a magnificent collection of art and antiquities. In Will's world, Lyra feigns interest in this museum and asks for directions, hoping to distract the police looking for her.

A view inside the courtyard of Exeter College, Philip Pullman's alma mater and model for the fictional Jordan College in His Dark Materials. In Lyra's world, Jordan College is "the grandest and richest" of the Oxford colleges with "buildings, which were grouped around three irregular quandrangles, dating from every period from the early Middle Ages to the mid-eighteenth century."

*An entrance to
the Botanic Garden*

BOOKS

Oxford, by John Curtis, is a collection of color photographs printed in landscape format, with paired quotations from books. Exeter College Hall merits a page, with its high timber roof, oil portraits on the walls, stained-glass windows, and two rows of dining tables with seats that serve this brightly lit hall. Ward Lock, in *A Pictorial and Descriptive Guide to Oxford,* writes that "The hall of Exeter College is a fine example of the open timber-roofed buildings of the kind . . . It contains some remarkable portraits."

Magdalen College, whose most prominent landmark is its famous Bell Tower, where Latin grace is sung on May Morning, attracting large crowds

A rooftop view of Exeter College from the University Church of St. Mary the Virgin

Might the hall have been an inspiration for the dining hall in Pullman's Jordan College? In the first chapter of *The Golden Compass,* Pullman writes: "The three great tables that ran the length of the hall were laid already, the silver and the glass catching what little light there was, and the long benches were pulled out ready for the guest. Portraits of former Masters hung high up in the gloom along the walls."

Houseboats at Jericho

A rooftop view of the city of Oxford

Houseboat at Jericho

Oxford, a Landmark Visitor's Guide by longtime Oxford resident Farrol Kahn, is an excellent tour book that explains everything you'd want to know about the city: its colorful history, its literary heritage, a walking tour of its colleges, and standard tourist information (lodging, retail stores, weather, cultural events, and so on). Illustrated with color photos, this pocket-sized guide is an excellent traveler's companion.

The Elements of His Dark Materials: A Guide to Philip Pullman's Trilogy, by Laurie Frost, details the many places in Oxford that have a parallel to Lyra's and Will's Oxford (see pages 215–241).

RECOMMENDED INTERNET SITES

http://en.wikipedia.org/wiki/Oxford • This is a detailed overview of the city, a good place to get an idea as to its historical heritage, its tourist attractions, its geography, and literary importance.

www.oxfordcity.co.uk • This is the official website for the city itself, with current information on lodging, food and drink, arts and entertainment, community, sport and leisure, shopping, home and garden, and so forth. Billing itself as a "mix of ancient and modern, there is plenty for both the tourist and the resident to do. Whether visiting one of the many historic buildings, college or museums, going out for a drink or a meal, taking in a show or shopping till you drop, Oxford has it all. . . ."

www.chem.ox.ac.uk/oxfordtour/sitemap.html • This is an especially useful site because it offers panoramic photos of the city's main attractions. (Note: Apple's QuickTime software is needed to view these 360-degree images.)

Radcliffe Camera: A famous landmark, this library is closed to the general public, though tours are available.

RECOMMENDED EVENTS

Oxford hosts an annual literary festival, sponsored by the *Sunday Times.* In March 2007, the city hosted its tenth Oxford Literary Festival, a six-day event that encompassed a wide range of literary interests, ranging from academic to popular culture.

This year, Philip Pullman made two appearances: to discuss the adaptation of a Sally Lockhart novel *(The Ruby in the Smoke),* and to discuss the adaptation of *The Golden Compass* to the silver screen.

Of special interest: There are several walking tours that a Pullman reader would find fascinating: Literary Oxford (two hours), a tour of the Bodleian Library (otherwise closed to the public),

The courtyard of Magdalen College

The entrance to the Sheldonian Theatre: Seating 1,500 patrons, this is one of the oldest theaters in the world.

and from the premiere bookseller in town, the Blackwell Literary Trail, the literature for which states: "[Led] by an experienced guide, this is an informative way of seeing Oxford: a literary tour which starts at the Festival bookshop and visits and references places where famous authors such as Jonathan Swift, Dorothy L. Sayers, J. R .R. Tolkien, T. E. Lawrence, C. S. Lewis, Philip Pullman, Alan Bennett and Iris Murdoch studied. The tour ends at the historic Blackwell bookshop at 50 Broad Street, founded in 1879 and boasting amongst its attractions the world-famous Norrington Room, which boasts over 160,000 volumes on three miles of shelving."

A rooftop view of Exexter College (foreground) and Radcliffe College (background)

While attending the festival, it's a good time to take advantage of the many walking tours that are sponsored by the Oxford Guild of Guides. Its main tour is "Oxford Past and Present," which gives a historical perspective; for the literary perspective, its themed tours include: Oxford Immortalised, Pottering in Harry's footsteps (Harry Potter), Alice in Oxford (Lewis Carroll), J. R. R. Tolkien, C. S. Lewis, and Philip Pullman.

Oxford is a city where dreamers dream, as Pullman explained in *Oxford Today:* "'Where do you get your ideas from?' is the commonest question writers get asked. The truthful answer is 'I dunno.' They just turn up. But when you're wandering about with your mouth open and your eyes glazed waiting for them to do so, there are few better places to wander about in than Oxford, as many novelists have discovered."

Rooftop view of Exeter College

The Sheldonian Theatre

The Hertford Bridge: Connecting two parts of Hertford College, the Bridge of Sighs (as it's informally known) was copied from the original in Venice.

KEY LOCATIONS OF INTEREST

Pullman was a long-time resident of Oxford, so it's not surprising that His Dark Materials, notably *The Golden Compass,* is replete with references to the city. Some are obvious, set in our world (Will's world); and some not so obvious (set in Lyra's world).

There are far too many Oxford references in His Dark Materials to be cited here, but following is a representative sampling, along with some other places of interest to those happily afflicted with bibliomania. For detailed information, consult Laurie Frost's exhaustive and definitive *Elements of His Dark Materials,* "Places and Peoples: The Oxfords."

Alchemy Boatyard • A boatyard in the Jericho area where canal barges are repaired, it is currently under consideration for replacement by a modern housing/retail development. Pullman adamantly opposes this effort and gave a statement to that effect. In Lyra's world, this is the home of the Gyptians, who befriend Lyra.

Bodleian Library • Fictionalized as Bodley's Library, where books can be found that tell one how to read the alethiometer, the Bodleian Library, with its ornate wooden door decorated with numerous coats of arms, is one of the most famous in the world. It houses almost seven million books that rest on 107 miles of shelves.

Botanic Garden (University of Oxford) • Founded in 1621, this garden is prominently and significantly featured in *The Amber Spyglass.* (To tell you more would be to give away too much of the story.)

Broad Street • A city of books, Oxford is a bibliophile's heaven. Any book lover will undoubtedly find himself haunting the bookstores on this street, most notably Blackwell's, cited by *Insight Compact Guide:*

A tree in the Botanic Garden

Oxford as "one of the world's most famous bookshops." Blackwell's, as you'd expect, is well stocked with books by and about Pullman.

Cherwell River • Located east of the city, near Magdalen College, this is where you can rent a punt (a low, shallow boat navigated by a long pole). In Lyra's world, it's a popular site for young children to bathe.

Christ Church • The home of the Oxford Literary Festival in 2007, Christ Church borders the Cherwell and Isis Rivers; Blackwell's is also nearby.

Eagle and Child (formerly Bird and Child) • Located on the corner of Wellington Place, this pub has a back room where members of the Inklings (J. R. R. Tolkien, C. S. Lewis, Charles Williams, and others) regularly met on Tuesday to drink beer and talk about anything, and everything, under the sun, moon, and stars.

Exeter College, University of Oxford • This is the model for Pullman's Jordan College. A graduate of Exeter, Pullman drew extensively on his recollections as an undergraduate, giving his books a rich and realistic background to serve as Lyra's world.

Institute of Archaeology • Located on Beaumont street, this place is visited by Will *(The Subtle Knife)* in his search for his father.

Norham Gardens • A residential road in central north Oxford, a popular place for the refined middle class. In Will's world *(The Subtle Knife)*, this is the street where the duplicitous Sir Charles Latrom (Lord Boreal) gives Lyra a lift and subsequently "lifts" her alethiometer.

There's also a photograph (one of four) of Norham Gardens in *Lyra's Oxford*: Addressed to Angela Gorman of Lancaster, England, the card is

Magdalen College

from Dr. Mary Malone, who writes that "it does show the place I work in and a house just around the corner from my flat. . . ."

Oxford [the town] • One of the most famous cities in the world, it is west-northwest of London (approximately fifty miles). In Will's world *(The Subtle Knife),* this is where he uses the subtle knife to enter Lyra's world by cutting a window.

Oxford [the university] • The university, comprising thirty-six colleges, counts 16,500 students. Exeter College, described by Farrol Kahn in *Oxford* as "the smallest and poorest of the medieval foundations" is transformed by Pullman into "the grandest and richest" of the twenty-four colleges in Lyra's world.

Pitt Rivers Museum • General Pitt Rivers founded the museum in 1884, initially donating 18,000 objects of archeological and ethnographic interest; the collection now totals more than a half million artifacts. According to its website (www.prm.ox.ac.uk), "The Pitt Rivers still retains its Victorian atmosphere. The cluttered cases, the original small handwritten labels and the absence of intrusive text-panels all contribute to the special experience it offers. Visitors interested in psychology, sociology, medicine, arts and crafts, comparative religion, music, in fact almost any profession or hobby, will find plenty to intrigue them. It is also a fascinating place for those studying changing historical attitudes."

In Will's world, this museum houses artifacts that are relevant in Dr. Mary Malone's study of Shadow-particles. It's also where Lyra, using her alethiometer, correctly identifies a trepanned skull on display as dating from 33,254 years (the card for this display incorrectly identifies it as from the Bronze Age).

Inside the Covered Market, the storefront of M. Feller, Son &
Daughter: Specialists in Organic Meats. The Covered Market consolidates
former stall holders into permanent shops, predominantly butchers.

In the Botanic Garden, a bench of special significance: It is where, in His Dark Materials, Lyra and Will meet annually in their respective worlds.

A view across the courtyard of Exeter College

Port Meadow • Residents of this area north and west of Oxford, familiar with Pullman's fictionalizing of it in His Dark Materials, sought and received Pullman's assistance in opposing the encroachment of a real estate developer who wanted to transform their neighborhood from its boat community to a complex of apartments and commercial shops. In a statement to the planning inquiry board, Pullman took exception to a barrister (representing Bellway Homes, the developer) who said this area was "a bit of an eyesore, it might be better if it was tidied away." Pullman pointed out that His Dark Materials, in fact, served as a draw for people worldwide who came "to see the places I wrote about—including the canal and the life around it." In other words, Pullman asserted that urban encroachment by Bellway Homes (or any other developer) was not in the best interests of the community.

Sunderland Avenue • This avenue, located in North Oxford, is where Will sees an open "window" cut in the air that allows Lyra and him to move between Cittagazze and Oxford. The hornbeam trees on this avenue serve as an identifying landmark as they move back and forth between the two worlds.

A rooftop view of Exeter College from the
University Church of St. Mary the Virgin

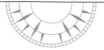

RANDOM THOUGHTS BY JOURNALISTS, CRITICS, READERS, AND FANS

PULLMAN AND CURIOSITY: "Pullman is a self-confessed magpie, who plucks ideas from all over the place—science, religion, poetry—then adds a twist. His angels, witches, humans and harpies exist against a convincing backdrop of parallel worlds and dark matter. The whole thing holds water largely because the science roots the fantasy. And it's no coincidence that the most honourable adult character in the trilogy is a scientist." (Celia Dodd, "Debate: Human nature: universally acknowledged," *Times Online,* May 8, 2004).

PULLMAN'S WRITING SHED: "They probably picture it as a kind of modest conservatory, set in sylvan splendor in some charmingly land-scaped garden. It isn't. It's a shed, the sort of shed where you'd expect to find a hoe and a hand mower and maybe the odd stick of rusty garden furniture, except here it's a cross between a madman's Tardis and Mr. Mole's home. A defunct computer is garlanded with artificial flowers, a life-sized stuffed wolf slavers under a posture chair and billions of little Post-it notes with exquisite handwriting on them are dotted about and BluTacked on all surfaces." (Sally Vincent, "Driven by dæmons," *Guardian,* Nov. 10, 2001)

CENSORSHIP AND *THE GOLDEN COMPASS*: "Amazon's Write Your Own Review notice boards feature some 800 contributions posted for the first volume alone, *The Golden Compass*. Some are by parents warning others to keep their children away, calling the books 'satanic' or 'dark and terrifying.' But considerably more come from rebellious readers in rural areas, aged from eleven to post-adolescence, many saying they were advised by parents not to read Pullman's work but ordered it by Internet and were duly captivated. They are also intrigued by how his stories view much of what they hear in Bible class through a different, vivid kaleido-scope." (Ed Vulliamy in New York, "Author puts Bible Belt to the test," *Observer*, Aug. 26, 2001)

POPULARITY OF HIS DARK MATERIALS: "In the seven years since [the] His Dark Materials trilogy first came out, it has quietly, without a gramme of hype, sold about a tenth of Harry Potter's total; figures which his most nearly comparable fellow authors (C. S. Lewis with the Narnia books and Tolkien with *Lord of the Rings*) took decades to build up to. As one literary editor said yesterday, adults read J. K. Rowling because she is not complicated; children like Pullman because he is. Hundreds of read-ers' reviews on amazon.co.uk bear that out." (John Ezard, "Fully booked," *Guardian Unlimited*, Jan. 24, 2002)

ON PULLMAN VS. ROWLING: "J. K. Rowling and Pullman together dominate children's fiction. This is a capricious market, and Pullman's stories are seen as intellectually sounder, the more heavyweight read in a world where children's fiction is read by adults. The film of His Dark Materials is being scripted by Tom Stoppard. And the play has just begun its run at the National Theatre in London—two parts, each three hours long. Last Saturday, I saw the first preview, playing to a packed Olivier Theatre. It is a beautiful production, the dæmons of the novels crisscrossing the stage with shafts of light, tissue paper creations lit from the inside." (Dina Rabinovitch, "His bright materials," *Guardian*, Dec. 10, 2003)

ON DÆMONS: "Your dæmon, according to Pullmanesque lore, is the creature of your deepest essence; a bird, reptile, insect or animal, attached to you by an inevitable thread, like an externalised soul. It is your guardian angel, your confidante, your conscience, your representa-tive. In childhood, when you make the choices that form your charac-ter, your dæmon changes; when you become an adult, it is what you have created, and it stays like that until you die. A slimy snake, a sly monkey, a fierce tiger, an obedient dog, a pussycat: it's yours. It's you." (Sally Vincent, "Driven by dæmons," *Guardian*, Nov. 10, 2001)

ON PUBLISHING SUCCESS: "Pullman has been publishing children's stories since he was twenty-five, but it took him three decades to be noticed and to make money. All that time, struggling on modest salaries in schools and at a teacher-training college, he was paying tithes in abundance to his craft." (John Cornwell, "Some enchanted author," *Sunday Times Magazine,* Oct. 24, 2004)

ON THE DIFFICULTIES OF WRITING THE FIRST CHAPTER OF *THE GOLDEN COMPASS:* "When he found Lyra, he finally found his storytelling voice. It took him ages to write the first chapter of *Northern Lights,* but after sixteen drafts, he was on safe ground at last. 'I'd never written in that tone before. It was sombre, it was cold, and there was a sense of spaciousness. I much prefer to be the omniscient narrator which is part of the old fairy-tale tradition and the nineteenth-century novel tradition: the thing Modernism got away from. Suddenly I had enormous freedom. I didn't expect that. You see, I'm not a fantasy fan. I'm uneasy to think I write fantasy." (Harriet Lane, "Pullman's progress," *Observer,* Oct. 10, 2004)

ON PUZZLEMENT ABOUT THE TITLE CHANGE FROM *NORTHERN LIGHTS* TO *THE GOLDEN COMPASS* IN THE U.S.: "I'm wondering why *Northern Lights* is called *The Golden Compass* in U.S. markets. Who decides these changes and how much say did you have in it? It seems to me that calling the amazing alethiometer a compass diminishes it and is misleading. Besides, the idea of the northern lights is enigmatic and alluring enough as it is. It also shortchanges and patronises U.S. readers in the same way as presuming that American Harry Potter readers were the only section of that readership who couldn't cope with a *Philosopher's Stone* and needed the dumbed-down *Sorcerer's Stone.*" (From an uncredited interviewer in "There has to be a lot of ignorance in me when I start a story," *Guardian,* Feb. 18, 2002)

ON PULLMAN WINNING THE WHITBREAD AWARD: "An author who has been shoved into a ghetto as just a children's entertainer had won one of the world's two highest book awards. In an extraordinary and probably short-lived shift in values, the judges gave the crown not to a novel set in the confines of contemporary Gloucestershire or Kilburn, but to a story grounded in alternative worlds: to a narrative which deals with love, moral conduct, power, nature, paradise, hell and the existence or otherwise of God, the universe and everything, some of the oldest themes of art." (John Ezard, "Fully booked," *Guardian,* Jan. 24, 2002)

107

ON PULLMAN'S FICTION: "Pullman country is no single place: he conjures parallel universes, like a possessed juggler. He is in command of the grand sweep and the tiniest of botanical details. I asked him about the world of the dead, which appears in the new book. Pullman proposes that each of us has 'a death' that goes with us through life 'a meek, pale chaperone.' His world of the dead is a terrible, understated, monochrome place." (Kate Kellaway, "A wizard with worlds," *Guardian,* Oct. 22, 2000)

ON PULLMAN'S BOOK COVERS: "People often wonder how book covers are picked, and fans of Philip Pullman are no different, so I asked him who picks his covers, and how they are chosen. Pullman explains that while he doesn't personally pick the covers, he believes they're of great importance in selling a book. His personal favorite is the cover of *Lyra's Oxford,* which he is very pleased with. Pullman also says that he now has some influence on the design of the books." (Ian Giles, "The Gothenburg Book Fair," 2005)

ON SCIENCE IN PULLMAN'S HIS DARK MATERIALS: "His Dark Materials may be the first fantasy series founded upon the ideals of the Enlightenment rather than upon tribal and mythic yearnings for kings, gods, and supermen. Pullman's heroes are explorers, cowboys, and physicists. The series offers an extended celebration of the marvels of science: discoveries and theories from the outer reaches of cosmology—about dark matter and the possible existence of multiple universes—and threaded into the story." (Laura Miller, "Far from Narnia," *New Yorker,* Dec. 12, 2005, and Jan. 2, 2006; posted online on Dec. 19, 2005)

ON FANTASY VERSUS REALITY IN PULLMAN'S FICTION: "This is why His Dark Materials is magic. What pulls me in and leaves me gasping is not the fantasy, but the reality—of the dizzying submersions of adolescence and the heartbreak of setting them aside. . . . Pullman's dæmons are what remind me what I was like, when everything in the world was still waiting to be done." (Julie Powell, "You must read this," NPR, Jan. 19, 2007)

SYNOPSIS OF *THE GOLDEN COMPASS* BY NEW LINE CINEMA'S PUBLICITY DEPARTMENT: "*The Golden Compass* tells the first story in Pullman's His Dark Materials trilogy. *The Golden Compass* is an exciting fantasy adventure, set in an alternative world where people's souls manifest themselves as animals, talking bears fight wars, and Gyptians and witches coexist. At the center of the story is Lyra, an eleven-year-old girl who starts out trying to rescue a friend who's been kidnapped by a mysterious organization known as the Gobblers—and winds up on an epic quest to save not only her world, but ours as well." (New Line Cinema movie synopsis)

ON PULLMAN'S NEWFOUND FAME REALIZED AFTER THE PUBLICATION OF *THE GOLDEN COMPASS*: "But there is a downside to fame—Pullman started feeling pestered: 'People didn't break into the shed, but the doorbell was always ringing, and I would open the door and find somebody standing there with a big pile of books and a big smile.' Now, says, Pullman, he has to be careful to limit his engagements. And, just to remind him, he has placed on a shelf a small skeleton with a sign attached saying: I said yes and I should have said no." (Writer uncredited, "The art of darkness," Telegraph.co.uk, March 11, 2003)

ON DÆMONS: "My friend Beth has been reading Pullman since she was eleven. She's fourteen now and still talks the metaphysical talk. She can give you the entire plot of the His Dark Materials trilogy, and knows that 'dæmon' is pronounced 'demon' and that we've all got one. Hers changes, she told me once. Sometimes it is a butterfly, sometimes a meerkat or a mongoose. When she grows up, it will be set. She hopes for a panther, or at least a lynx. But not a dog. Only servants have dogs. There was no point asking her what a dæmon is. She'd throw her eyes heavenwards: 'You know, it's your thing. The thing you have.'" (Sally Vincent, "Driven by dæmons," *Guardian*, Nov. 10, 2001)

ON BLUTACK AND POST-IT NOTES: "BluTack plays a big part in Philip Pullman's writing process. With it he sticks to the wall pictures, notes, posters, reminders, postcards, book jackets, anything that will stay there. Another product of technology that Philip can't do without is Post-it notes, the smallest yellow ones in particular. They are very useful for planning the shape of a story: he writes a brief sentence summarising a scene on one of them, and then puts them on a very big piece of paper which he can fill with up to sixty or more different scenes, moving them around to get the best order." (From a biographical sketch on teenreads.com)

ON PULLMAN AND CHRISTIANITY: "If Lewis was a preacher [in the Narnia books], Pullman is one all the more—only in the service of a different religion. It's the faith of the Enlightenment, of scientific materialism, of secular values and truths that are fluid, of republics rather than kingdoms." (Alicia Mosier, quoted by Gina R. Dalfonzo in "The impoverished imagination," www.breakpoint.org)

Gyptian Narrowboat

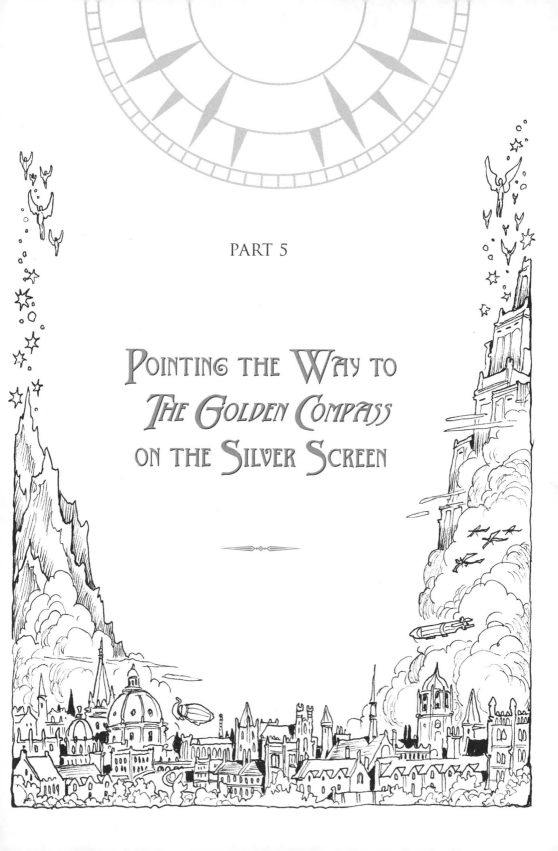

PART 5

Pointing the Way to
The Golden Compass
on the Silver Screen

Note: As producer Deborah Forte said during a roundtable discussion at the Oxford Book Festival in 2007, exposition is death to a movie. The key to a movie is showing, not telling. So how can you adequately explain on-screen what a dæmon is? What Dust is? And what an alethiometer is?

Here's a short overview that will point you in the right direction.

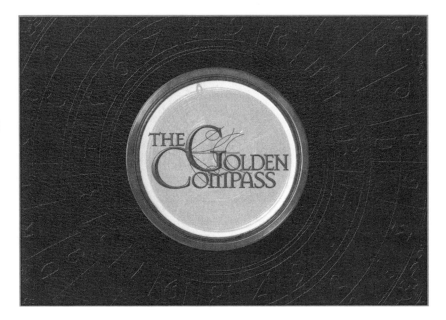

A close-up of the cover of the **The Golden Compass**
pressbook (12 x 17 inches), published by New Line Cinema

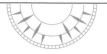

Dæmons

ne of the more intriguing concepts Pullman came up with when crafting His Dark Materials is his literary invention of the dæmon. Not to be confused with a demon—an evil spirit that haunts humankind—the dæmon is a person's soul in external form.

Here's what we are told about dæmons.

1. A dæmon has its own name.

2. A dæmon is almost always the opposite sex of its counterpart, a human. Theirs is a symbiotic relationship.

3. A dæmon can take the form of an insect, a bird, a reptile, or a mammal.

4. When the human counterpart is young, a dæmon can change its form at will and, in doing so, assumes the new form's attributes; that is, once transformed into a bird, a dæmon can fly.

5. A dæmon will eventually become fixed in its form. This is called "settling." Because its final form reflects a person's character, its final form is not a matter of choice. Some examples: soldiers = wolves; servants = dogs; witches = birds. For example, the treacherous Lord Boreal's dæmon is a snake; the majestic and untamed Lord Asriel's is an exotic creature, a snow leopard; the beguiling, manipulative Mrs. Coulter's is an exotic golden monkey; and Lyra's is (most often) an ermine, in part inspired by Leonardo da Vinci's *Lady with an Ermine*.

6. A dæmon dies when its human counterpart dies. At the moment of death, a dæmon simply discorporates and vanishes.

7. The connection between a dæmon and its counterpart is so strong that to be physically separated by more than a few feet causes pain: the greater the separation, the greater the corresponding pain.

8. It is taboo to touch another person's dæmon. (In His Dark Materials, when a soldier seizes Lyra's dæmon, she is horribly shocked and feels intimately violated.)

9. The connection between a person and his or her dæmon is so strong that severing it releases a tremendous amount of energy. This energy is the subject of great interest to all concerned: Lord Asriel, seeking to bridge the gap between his world and the other world hidden in the Aurora Borealis; Mrs. Coulter who runs the Oblation Board where experiments in "intercision" (severing the person from his/her dæmon) are being conducted for their so-called scientific value; and the omnipresent church in Lyra's world that seeks to hold on to its power at all costs.

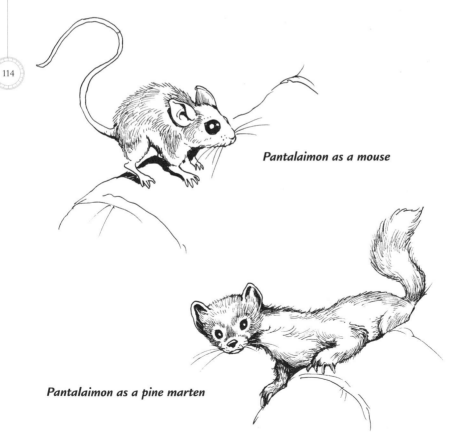

Pantalaimon as a mouse

Pantalaimon as a pine marten

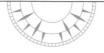

Dust

FOR DUST THOU ART, AND UNTO DUST SHALT THOU
RETURN.

—Genesis 3:19

ust, with a capital "D," is at the heart of His Dark
Materials.

In *The Golden Compass,* we become aware of its existence and its importance, when Lord Asriel shows photographs (which
he calls photograms) of Dust to a group of scholars at Jordan College,
who react with astonishment. The purpose of Lord Asriel's visit is to
finance further research into the nature of Dust: what it is, where it
comes from, what it does, and what can be done (if anything) to control
it.

In *The Subtle Knife,* we learn of the importance of Dust, called "dark
matter," which we're told is the subject of examination by Dr. Mary
Malone, who terms it "Shadows" or "Shadow-particles."

In *The Amber Spyglass,* we learn of the nature of Dust, and its critical
importance to not only Lyra's world but the millions of parallel worlds,
as well.

Dust was originally named Rusakov Particles after its discoverer, an
experimental theologian named Boris Mikhailovitch Rusakov of
Muscovy (in Lyra's world, the counterpart to what we know as Russia).
Dust cannot be seen by the naked eye; a filtering device like the amber
spyglass must be used to detect it. (It can be photographed, however,
with the right photographic film emulsions.)

Dust is attracted to adults, especially young adults nearing puberty.
As to what Dust actually is, two angels (Balthamos and Xaphania)
provide useful explanations. In *The Amber Spyglass,* Balthamos says of

Dust: "Only a name for what happens when matter begins to under-stand itself. Matter loves matter. It seeks to know more about itself, and Dust is formed." Xaphania says, "Conscious beings make Dust—they renew it all the time, by thinking and feeling and reflecting, by gaining wisdom and passing it on."

The angels, we are told, were formed when Dust became conscious of itself; and the first angel, the Authority, convinced other angels that he in turn created them and all the worlds, as well. But as the Authority aged, weakening as he lapsed into senility, he appointed another angel, Metatron, to be his right hand; Metatron is his regent in the Kingdom of Heaven.

In Lyra's world, the Magisterium considers Dust to be original sin. Dust, to those who control the church, is something not to be respected but feared and therefore controlled. Alarmingly, Dust is leaving all the worlds—it's leaking out through holes cut by the subtle knife and through the inadvertent consequences of human actions.

Emma Raynaud

*Like a Gyptian narrowboat, this is a houseboat
moored at Jericho at the end of Oxford Canal.*

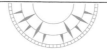

The Alethiometer

orthern Lights, the original title of the first of three novels comprising His Dark Materials, is the title used for the U.K. edition; however, the U.S. edition bears a different title, *The Golden Compass,* which has led to considerable confusion. With the release of New Line Cinema's film adaptation, also titled *The Golden Compass,* newcomers will likely be perplexed, wondering what exactly *Northern Lights* is, and where it fits in with His Dark Materials.

Adding to the uncertainty: It's well known that the principal inspiration for His Dark Materials is an epic poem by John Milton called *Paradise Lost,* in which the following lines (Book VII, lines 225–227) appear:

He took the golden compasses, prepared

In God's eternal store, to circumscribe

This universe, and all created things.

This may have some bearing on why the U.S. publisher of His Dark Materials thought to retitle the book from *Northern Lights* to *The Golden Compass.*

Upon reflection, I think Pullman's original title is the better of the two. The northern lights is a reference to an unusual celestial phenomenon visible in the northern regions, a wavering ribbon of light; its color varies in hue and intensity depending on its altitude: green (highest), blue and purple (midrange), and red (low).

In chapter 2 of *The Golden Compass,* Lord Asriel is addressing scholars at the Retiring Room of Jordan College, and the subject at hand is Dust and, of course, the Northern Lights.

Just as the mention of the northern lights opens *The Golden Compass,*

117

things come full circle as its appearance concludes the book, setting the stage for *The Subtle Knife*.

When the U.S. publisher decided on retitling the book *The Golden Compass*, the question arises: What, exactly, *is* the Golden Compass? We find the answer in chapter 4 of the book, when the Master of Jordan College gives Lyra a gift. It's "a thick disc of gold and crystal. It might have been a compass or something of the sort."

As it turns out, it's clearly *not* a compass that points to specific directions. Lyra's gift is an alethiometer, a handheld mechanical object that tells the truth. Invented, Pullman tells us, by a seventeenth-century scholar named Pavel Khunrath who lived in Prague, the number of alethiometers in the world can be counted on two hands. According to the Master, there are only six known devices in the world—probably a good estimate, since there are four in the hands of people discussed in *His Dark Materials*: Lyra (obviously), Pavel, Teukros Basilides (who works for Lord Asriel), and the alethiometrist for the Society of the Work of the Holy Spirit.

Unlike a compass, which uses the Earth's magnetic fields to point its needle, an alethiometer uses four hands that point to the thirty-six symbols that surround its face: three winding wheels control the shorter hands, each fixed in place; the fourth hand, the longest, swings freely, wavers, but doesn't settle.

The alethiometer is Pullman's invention, drawing its inspiration from Greek mythology, specifically, the river Lethe in Hades. Drinking from this river causes forgetfulness. Interestingly, the Greek word for "truth" is *alethia*, so Pullman's alethiometer is a device that measures truth.

As Fra Pavel, who has an alethiometer, explains, it "does not *forecast*" but "*if* certain things come about, *then* the consequences will be" what they will be. In other words, a reading is conditional; the future timeline is in a state of perpetual flux, affecting the reading itself.

With the alethiometer in hand, Lyra is able to navigate her way successfully through a number of situations that might have turned out differently had she relied only on Pantalaimon, blind luck, or her own plucky personality.

A pamphlet about the alethiometer and its use, written by Pullman and published by the National Theatre, explains not only the history of the alethiometer but how to properly use it; on the back, in color, is a twelve-by-fifteen-inch close-up of the alethiometer, with all its symbols clearly visible, and detailed notes as to what they symbolize. (Unfortunately, this instructive pamphlet is out of print.)

For those who wish to try their hand reading an alethiometer, the official movie website for *The Golden Compass* (www.goldencompassmovie.com) hosts one for your manipulation. (A bonus: If you pick the right combinations, it will reveal conceptual art for the movie that otherwise remains hidden.)

For those who wish to have in hand a replica of the alethiometer, inexpensive toy replicas are available from Corgi.

119

The alethiometer as depicted in a fold-out brochure (11.75 x 16.5 inches) published by the National Theatre in conjunction with its production of Philip Pullman's His Dark Materials

$\mathcal{T}$HE $\mathcal{G}$OLDEN $\mathcal{C}$OMP$\mathcal{ASS}$: FROM $\mathcal{B}$OOK TO $\mathcal{S}$CREEN

 go to the official movie website for *The Golden Compass* and navigate my way to the page that has a functional alethiometer. I pose a question: "Will the film version of *The Golden Compass* meet the expectations of fans worldwide and be successful enough to justify continuing this film franchise?" I set its three red hands and then the main hand swivels and points to:

> The first symbol: achieved wisdom, alchemy, craft
> The second symbol: sovereignty, politics, fame
> The third symbol: nourishment, sacrifice

Pullman tells us in "How to read the Alethiometer" that each symbol "supplies the semantic content of a message," but it is "the mind of the inquirer [that] supplies the grammatical connections between the individual elements. Only when the two work together does the full meaning become apparent."

Here's how I read the symbols:

The first symbol speaks of Pullman's dedication to his craft and his realization that writing success would have to be earned, not prematurely realized, hence his long apprenticeship before finding the success he sought. At age fifty, after three decades of publishing books, he was able to become a full-time writer. He had achieved wisdom in those years, culminating in his greatest work to date, His Dark Materials.

The second symbol speaks of the film industry and its dominance in the entertainment arts. We live in an increasingly visual society. (Don't all newspapers now look like *USA Today*?) It's also the seductive world of film that holds our attention. Book festivals, book reviews, and book awards all pale in comparison to the glitzy, glamorous worlds of television and film that have captivated a bedazzled, starstruck public. Ironically, the writer who creates the work is largely anonymous, though the world he creates and the words mouthed by actors in the film belong to him and the screenwriter. No matter. Fame is the province of the actors, who to the adoring public will always be the center of attention. Writers are, and will always be, relatively anonymous to the moviegoing public.

Great forces, though, are at work: A politic decision must be made by studio executives, who are always mindful of the bottom line. What will the film cost to produce, and what profits will result? To be "politic" means to be "shrewd or prudent in practical matters; tactful; diplomatic." All of these come into play as New Line, wishing it had its own alethiometer, committed to bring *The Golden Compass* to the silver screen. But, lacking a working alethiometer, New Line relies on the track record of the book, its strong storyline, and the heady prospect of repeating the success it enjoyed with *The Lord of the Rings* film franchise.

Finally, the third symbol: nourishment, sacrifice. New Line realizes that the success of *The Golden Compass* can only be achieved if the film version is faithful to the book.

Once the decision was made to go ahead (or in Hollywood parlance, the project was green-lit), $150 million was earmarked for the first of three films, starting with *The Golden Compass*. Its budget matched that of *The Chronicles of Narnia: The Lion, the Witch, and the Wardrobe*. In many ways, *His Dark Materials: The Golden Compass* would prove just as challenging. From finding the right girl to play Lyra—the key role for the success of this film series—to finding the perfect couple to be cast as her parents, the challenges were considerable. A newcomer, Dakota Blue Richards, was cast in the leading role as Lyra Belacqua. Backing her up were British actor Daniel Craig (as Lord Asriel) and Australian actress Nicole Kidman (as Mrs. Coulter) in their critical roles as her parents.

With all the symbols provided by the alethiometer carefully considered, buttressed by my aforementioned years of study at Jordan College where I majored in symbology, I conclude that the film adaptation of *The Golden Compass* will be a critical and financial success, that fans (old and new alike) will be entranced by the film and the story of Lyra and her allies, and that New Line will proceed apace with the second in the series, *The Subtle Knife*, to premiere in 2009 (my educated guess).

In truth, it doesn't take a golden compass to know that the film will be a box office success. New Line Cinema took no chances and got the word out early. In the spring of 2007, well before the film's release on December 7,

New Line Cinema erected an impressive, eye-catching website with Flash animation, issued an elaborate press book (twelve by seventeen inches, in full color with an elegant cover), hosted a London premiere for journalists with a personal tour of the studio, and published a limited edition, 155-page "cast and crew" hardback book of 1,000 copies.

Not surprisingly, New Line followed the playbook it used to promote *The Lord of the Rings,* hoping to get the kind of buzz that, to use a Tolkien phrase, would set tongues wagging in Hobbiton.

Predictably, New Line's concerted efforts worked. Joblo.com's Jenny Karakaya got the full tour on a press junket and came away impressed. "Based on the footage and scenes, Dakota Blue Richards captures the essence of the innocent Lyra quite effectively, thus making the gamble of the open casting call worthwhile. Kidman and Craig are remarkable, while Pullman's imagination is realized with a genuine recreation of a multifaceted and philosophical world. The cinematography is quite beautiful, with enhanced vivid colors that give a realism and authenticity to this alternate, fantasy universe in *The Golden Compass.*"

Is it too early to talk about multiple Oscar nominations for *The Golden Compass*? Susan Wloszczyna of *USA Today* doesn't think so. After looking down the road, she cites *His Dark Materials: The Golden Compass* as a film with Oscar potential.

At this writing, nine months before the movie debut, the film buzz is active and increasing with each passing month. Already, the mighty merchandising engine—the tie-in books, the toys, the collectibles—is being cranked up, with plush dolls, action figures, trading cards, movie replicas, and movie-related books in the works. The forthcoming holidays will see *Golden Compass*–related products under Christmas trees everywhere, if the licensees get their holiday wish. After all, what kid can resist having Pantalaimon as a plush toy? Or a Lyra doll?

Not to put too fine a point on it, but the movie will likely be praised as the next initial offering of the next great film franchise for fantasy fans; and all the time, money, and effort put into taking the book to film will surely be investments that will pay off, as New Line Cinema forges on with *The Subtle Knife* and *The Amber Spyglass.*

The important thing to remember, though, is that the success of the film will attract millions of filmgoers (that is, new readers) to the books, which is where the real richness of Lyra's story can be experienced. And that, to my mind, is a good and wonderful thing. As wonderful as the film will likely be, the books are unquestionably a deeper, richer experience.

123

The Golden Compass had its roots in a small but comfortable garden shed in Pullman's backyard, where he wrote all three of the books that comprise His Dark Materials. "It's a twelve feet by eight wooden shed and it's been up for ten years. It's insulated and heated. The chaos and filth and mess in there are indescribable and it's crammed with books and manuscripts; I can never find anything in there—I'm ashamed of it. I go down there every morning and generally write three pages by lunchtime, always by hand," he wrote in *Talking Books*.

That shed, described as "grubby . . . the fly-blown awfulness of it— the cobwebs, the dusty bric-a-brac, the masks, the posters and children's drawings, the defunct computer garlanded in plastic flowers, the faded flowery curtain, the giant six foot fluffy rat" (as the *Telegraph* described it) is where *The Golden Compass* took seed and blossomed: Twelve years later, the fruits of New Line's labor will bring Pullman's story to a world-wide audience and, it is hoped, leave them gasping, anxious to explore Lyra's enchanting, magical world.

Tiffany Vincent

A functional pocket watch with the symbols of the alethiometer, a one-of-a-kind artifact created by Tiffany Vincent

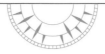

Philip Pullman at the Oxford Literary Festival 2007

Transcribed by Nicola Priest

elebrating its tenth anniversary, the Oxford Literary Festival was held in March 2007 at Christ Church, one of the largest colleges at Oxford. This year, the star attraction was Philip Pullman who, in the company of film producer Deborah Forte and visual effects supervisor Michael Fink, talked to a crowd of 600 people about how *The Golden Compass* was adapted from book to film. After the talk, they answered questions from the audience and made themselves available to sign books and movie memorabilia.

Chaired by Mark Lawson, the panel discussion of *The Golden Compass* took place on March 24, 2007.

————⟫◈⟪————

Mark Lawson: Philip, can we begin by talking about your inspiration for the books?

Philip Pullman: Landscapes of Hell in *Paradise Lost* by Milton was a starting point. The fire, darkness, and wild landscapes—I really wanted to steal that. Also, the works of William Blake. I certainly didn't expect that *The Golden Compass* would ever be made into a film. I expected just a few hundred readers and I am astonished at its success.

Deborah Forte: I first read the story in manuscript form. I spend a lot of my time reading manuscripts. I was looking for that special work. I thought this book would make the most beautiful film because it's so visual and compelling. I thought wherever Philip is going, I want to go with him. My background is in publishing. The challenge was to make a film that would live up to the promise of the books. As readers, you really owned Philip's story in your mind's eye. I have to translate that to a communal experience and to live up to the promise that the writer has given to the readers. It's a very big undertaking.

Only two percent of auctioned manuscripts actually get made into films. I credit New Line. It's because of their vision that this film is being made at all. This project has been twelve years in development. But I waited until the trilogy was completed before finding a studio and financial partners.

I had lunch with Philip when he was writing *The Amber Spyglass*. I asked Philip how the trilogy was going to end. He said, "Imagine how boring the world would have been if Eve had not taken a bite of the apple."

Mark Lawson: You did have a change of scriptwriter on the film. Is that right?

Deborah Forte: It isn't uncommon on big films to have several writers. If you look at the credits, some big films have seven or eight writers. We had two: Tom Stoppard and Chris Weitz. When you develop a script, it cannot have all the narrative of the novel because you have to tell the story in a condensed way.

Philip Pullman: I liked what Tom Stoppard wrote, but the studio didn't.

Deborah Forte: Communication is key, as all the characters belong to Philip. All the interactions and communications I've had with Philip have been rich and plentiful. It was always about sticking with Lyra, to focus on her.

It was important for us to know what was sacrosanct. We needed to be sensitive to Philip's concepts and themes; it's easy to get sidetracked. Sometimes you can fall in love with a scene but know that you're unable to execute it. It's a push-pull situation. So the script must be carefully managed to tell the story but remain true to the book and the vision.

You then have to deliver on the promise of the script. It's not one person; there are several team captains in charge of bringing the film to the screen. Dennis Gassner, the production designer, was the first of those team captains to come on board. He toured Oxford, he went to museums, and he hired a team of conceptual artists and began to put images together. It was a very exciting time. The studio has been very supportive in helping to deliver a very ambitious project.

Philip Pullman: It has been fascinating to watch the process develop. As a novelist, I knew nothing of the film world. As it turned out, they had all read the books. I was surprised to learn that this is not always the case! But they have the vision in their minds. I have been very impressed that all the production team understands the concept of the books, that they are about Lyra and her parents.

Deborah Forte: When Philip Pullman came to the movie set, it was like having a rock star on board. Everyone was asking, "What time will Mr. Pullman be on set?" Philip had a wonderful visit with the props master. He had a team of 120 people working with him making the props, and Philip was really interested in the forge. All of these people wanted to have their work live up to Philip's approval and validation.

Mark Lawson: **Let's talk about the casting for this film. This is the first fantasy film with A-list stars.**
Philip Pullman: Well, I wouldn't say that to Ian McKellen.

Mark Lawson: **He's a great actor, but I wouldn't really say he was an A-list star.[2] What was your dream casting?**
Philip Pullman: Nicole Kidman and Sir Laurence Olivier circa 1945, but he was not available. The ambition was not to find the movie stars, but to find the best actors for the roles. Nicole Kidman has amazing versatility; she can be warm and cold, seductive and terrifying at the same time. It was also essential to get Lyra right. I didn't know how they were going to do it, but they did get it right.
Deborah Forte: We all agreed it should be a young person who would come into the role and be naive and who could grow throughout the film. New Line recognised that Lyra needed to be someone with very little acting experience, which is a big risk for studios because Lyra's is the main role.

We saw 10,000 girls in open auditions. The casting agents did a good job. The first casting session held in Cambridge was the most promising. A DVD was made of the prospective candidates, the best forty girls. Philip viewed that DVD. Forty-eight hours later he said, "It's one of two girls." Dakota Blue Richards was one of those two.

Mark Lawson: **The current James Bond, Daniel Craig, will be playing Lord Asriel?**
Deborah Forte: He is a brilliant actor. He has a presence that makes you watch him on the screen. I saw him in *Layer Cake* and he was great. He had a ruthless streak in that film, which Lord Asriel also has.

Mark Lawson: **Yes, there is a bit of history with James Bond, as Timothy Dalton, who played James Bond in *License to Kill* and *The Living Daylights,* played Lord Asriel in the first run of the theatre production.**

---

[2]British actor Ian McKellen played Gandalf in *The Lord of the Rings*. I don't think he'd be pleased by Lawson's assertion.

Philip Pullman: Both Nicole Kidman and Daniel Craig are brilliant actors.

Mark Lawson: **It must have been daunting for Dakota Blue Richards to have her first acting day with Nicole Kidman and Daniel Craig.**

Deborah Forte: Daniel met Dakota on the first day of filming, which was in the Exeter College gardens. I knew she was a little nervous. Just before they were about to shoot, he started smiling at her and then he began jumping up and down on the spot to make her laugh. Dakota didn't know what to do; she looked up at him in bewilderment and then she just mimicked him. So they were both jumping up and down on the spot. It really put her at ease, physically relaxing her.

Mark Lawson: **We'll move on to the visual effects. Mike, that is particularly challenging with this film, isn't it?**

Mike Fink: It's one of the big challenges.

Deborah Forte: The visual effects are more subtle than, say, *The Lord of the Rings* because of the dæmons. Mike's job is to make it look real. He has to do what words do in the book, but in film it has to be done through pictures.

Mike Fink: There are three people responsible for the teams bringing the words to the screen: the director of photography, the production designer, and myself. I've worked for thirty years just to make this movie. Unfortunately, it is too early to show complete footage from the film itself. I'm going to show you some footage of films I've worked on to give you an idea of my background. By the way, when I say "I," what I really mean is a team of one thousand people.

[Mike shows footage from *Constantine*.]

Mike Fink: The inspiration for the vision of Hell in this movie is a nuclear blast shockwave that just goes on forever.

[The next clips are from *X-Men* and *X-Men 2*. Mike shows clips of *Night Crawler, Mystique,* and *Magneto*.]

Mike Fink: This is the scene where Magneto (played by Ian McKellen) is imprisoned in a cage. Everything in the picture, apart from the actor, is completely synthesised.

Now we do have some clips from *The Golden Compass*. Although they're only about ten percent finished, it'll give you the sense of the scale. This is the visual manufacturing process for the ship. The ship is CGI [computer-generated imagery], but water and camera angles came from filming a ship on the ocean. Water is too difficult and time consuming to synthesise otherwise. This is the ship arriving at Trollesund. The ship on the sea tells the tale through pictures of Lyra traveling. It's an exercise that takes up a lot of text to describe but can be done almost instantly in moving images.

[Mike shows clips of the ship's transition from its initial CG model and through various stages in the process.]

Mike Fink: We did a lot of research into the animals for the dæmons. For example, when Pan takes the form of a ferret, we studied ferrets with extra high-definition film, so the camera can zoom in on the fur. This one is Pan as a mouse.

[Mike shows footage of real animals filmed for research purposes.]

Mike Fink: This was then translated into CG models, the fur rendered, and animation tests undertaken. We don't want them to look like visual effects. This process ensures that the dæmons will look organic.

[The creation and movement of Stelmaria, various other dæmons, a concept sketch of the London skyline, and Mrs. Coulter's sky ferry are shown.]

Mike Fink: All of our work in progress on the London scenes is based on the concept sketch by Dennis Gassner, the production designer.

Mark Lawson: **Have Harry Potter and *The Lord of the Rings* made it easier for studios to understand this film?**

Deborah Forte: Perhaps, but it is most important that the film lives up to the book's reputation. Historically, we had a conversation where the film does not begin with Lyra and Pan as in the book. There are much bigger set pieces in the book, which could have been a starting point and a more gradual way to get into her story. But it was felt that it was critical to explain the human-dæmon relationship as soon as possible. If left to later in the film, it would have taken too long to explain. Exposition is death to a movie.

Philip Pullman: Yes, exposition could kill the flow of the narrative. It's about Lyra; it begins and ends with her.

Mark Lawson: **What about the film's antireligion theme?**

Philip Pullman: Not antireligion, but antioppression, antiauthoritarian. It's opposed to the use of theocracy for political gain. The Church in Lyra's world is very different from our own, as many things are.

Deborah Forte: I feel the story's main concept themes are love, courage, responsibility, and honour.

Mark Lawson: **But the story dramatises the death of God?**

Deborah Forte: Not the death of God but the death of oppressive authority.

AUDIENCE QUESTIONS

Q: **Having read the trilogy, I was very excited to hear that the film is being made. How can you convey the beauty of the books in film? How does the film compare to the theatrical performances of His Dark Materials?**

Philip Pullman: Theatre works by metaphor. In theatre productions, we have to pretend more, as we do not have the facility to convey all of the visual images on stage. Actors wear animal masks for the dæmons and the audience pretends they can't see the actors. There are more constraints in theatre, such as the theatregoer's purse or the length of time the human back can bear. The production took place in two rather than three parts, as they needed to show all of the production in one day. Nicholas Wright made two shows each lasting three hours. I liked the production a lot, particularly the music; the music played in the Land of the Dead sends shivers down my spine when I just think about it.

It's different from the processes involved in bringing the story to film. It's a very different thing altogether. Whilst the constraints of production and expectations of the audience are very different, there is no better studio than New Line to produce it.

Q: **How do you feel about the change of title from the original *Northern Lights* to *The Golden Compass*?**

Philip Pullman: Before I settled upon His Dark Materials for the trilogy, the working title was *The Golden Compasses,* again taken from Milton's *Paradise Lost.* It refers to a pair of compasses. These same God's golden compasses can also be found in William Blake's work. The editor at the publishers in New York thought I was referring to the alethiometer and they wanted to use *The Golden Compass* as the title for the book in the United States.

In many countries, the first book was published under the name *The Golden Compass,* so this is how most people across the world recognise it. In fact, that same editor was responsible for changing *Harry Potter and the Philosopher's Stone,* which makes sense, into *Harry Potter and the Sorcerer's Stone,* which does not.

Q: **Are you pleased with the film so far?**

Philip Pullman: I'm very pleased with everything I've seen. People seem to want argument and confrontation to develop, but I could not be more pleased with it. The casting is terrific, and we have definitely found the right Lyra. The story has been treated with great respect. The visual effects are brilliant, and the costumes and sets are all very faithful to the story.

Q: **It was reported that the director, Chris Weitz, pulled out of the film. If so, how did you persuade him to come back?**
Deborah Forte: We gave him a second chance. We convinced him and he realised his mistake.

Q: **Would the first book be different if the two later books had not been written?**
Philip Pullman: I may have liked to change some parts of the story retrospectively, particularly from the first book. But with film, you have the luxury of looking ahead and adapting the story accordingly.

Q: **What is your favourite scene of the film so far?**
Philip Pullman: I have two favourite scenes. The first is when Lyra first meets Iorek Byrnison. The second scene is a quiet, but beautiful scene, which takes place on Lee Scoresby's balloon. It's Lee and Serafina Pekkala talking while Lyra is asleep. They are flying into danger and share that time of quiet comfort and inevitability together. The mood is very accurate to the book.

131

Q: **The Mulefa are not shown in the theatrical production. Why? Will they be shown in the film?**
Philip Pullman: There are some things you can do on stage and some you can't. It would have been difficult to have those creatures trundling along on wheels on a stage. It was the same with the witches. It's practically impossible to have several witches on wires flying around everywhere on stage. Wires would cross over, get tangled, and the whole thing would end up very messy. Also, you cannot easily convey the vast space and landscape on stage. In film, you can have vast panoramic shots of landscape.
Deborah Forte: We went to Svalbard to shoot some amazing landscapes to help bring the audience into the film. The film does have flying witches on wires—airbrushed out, of course. The costumes for the witches are wonderful, really colourful and ethereal.

Q: **How will Dust be portrayed in the film?**
Mike Fink: With great difficulty! It's difficult to explain, but the process of its appearance and interaction will be very carefully developed.

Q: Have you ever been asked to produce a visual effect that you couldn't do?

Mike Fink: Only once. The director asked me if I could do it and I said I didn't think so. I got a physicist from a German company to research if it was possible. I don't really want to explain the visual effect because it's complicated and I want to keep this short. I ended up giving up after a lot of time and effort. But with enough time and money now, there is nothing we cannot show. But this is not important; instead, it's important to be true to the concept of the story.

Deborah Forte: It appears that technology has caught up with Philip's imagination. The film may have been quite disappointing had it have been made six years ago.

Q: Some of the audience will know every word of the book; other cinemagoers will not have read the story. Is it difficult to cater to such different audiences?

Deborah Forte: As long as we follow the roadmap of the true story, we hope to appeal to all.

Q: You began to write these books several years ago. Do you feel like you're stuck in a time warp as you have to revisit the story over and over?

Philip Pullman: I'm writing my new novel, *The Book of Dust*. That's my priority.

His Dark Materials has been revisited in several formats and settings. It's been through several incarnations: the audiobooks, the plays, and now the film. This story's been around a bit. I'm very fortunate and flattered that people want to make my novels into films. I'm confident it will do well in film.

Q: In the book, there are some graphic scenes such as the dæmon separation scene. What audience are you aiming at? What film certification do you think the film will be given, a 12A rating[3] or a PG rating?

Philip Pullman: I cannot predict what the audience is going to be.

Deborah Forte: I'm not sure what rating the film will be given. We must make the best film we can out of the story.

Mark Lawson: But surely there are financial implications. You do have some power with that. If the Film Board came back with a 15 rating,[4] you could recut the film. Would you do that?

Deborah Forte: Yes, a 15 rating would be damaging.

---

[3]A British Board of Film Classification: "Suitable for those aged 12 and over; those aged under 12 are only admitted if accompanied by an adult."

[4]A British Board of Film Classification: "Suitable for those aged 15 and over."

Q: Are there any bits in the book that won't be in the film?

Philip Pullman: Yes. All my beautiful prose! No, no, all of the essential elements are there. When I read the novels aloud for the audiobooks, it took eleven hours. So you have to cut it, but it's not as drastic as it might seem. There is a lot of description in the novel, but it will just be done with visuals in the film.

Q: Where are you up to with the sequel *The Book of Dust*? Could you tell us what it's about?

Philip Pullman: It's about Dust. It's not really a sequel. The main character will be Lyra, of course, and she will be a bit older. But I don't really want to say too much more than that yet. I'm well into the story, but I've had a lot of interruptions. It will be published in two years or so.

Q: When you began writing the first book, did you know it was going to be a trilogy?

Philip Pullman: Not precisely, but I knew it was going to be a long story of at least one thousand pages. It's difficult to get a book of that size published unless you're a famous author. The story divided itself naturally into three parts, so that's how it was published. And that's how *The Lord of the Rings* is divided, of course.

Q: Why did you call your main character Lyra?

Philip Pullman: Because she was Lyra to me from the very beginning. I didn't have to work on it, but with other characters, I did. For example, I had to work out Iorek Byrnison because he was from the north and he had to have a Nordic-sounding name. It was the same with the witch Serafina Pekkala, which I got from the Helsinki [Sweden] phone book.

Mark Lawson: Really? One person's name or a combination?

Philip Pullman: It was two separate people.

Q: With child actors growing up fast, what stage are you in the scripts for *The Subtle Knife* and *The Amber Spyglass*?

Deborah Forte: We have a screenwriter writing the script for the second film and outlining the plot of the third.

Q: Did you write the books with an awareness of cinema?

Philip Pullman: I think every novelist in the past one hundred years has written with an awareness of cinema. If you look at the works of Charles Dickens, however, his panoramic impressions of a city are cinematic. If you read the opening to *Bleak House,* it's a shooting script, with an

133

awareness of writing with a sort of fluidity. So it hasn't changed very much. It's something that's inspired me a great deal. I've also stolen a great deal from Milton and from every book I've ever read. But I did acknowledge the other works at the end of *The Amber Spyglass.*

Q: Do you remember the moment when you first had the idea for the dæmons?

Philip Pullman: Yes, I was on the sixteenth draft of the first chapter. Raymond Chandler, an American detective writer once said, "When in doubt, have a man come through a door with a gun in his hand." It moves the story on like nothing else. Pantalaimon is my gun. I realised I needed someone for Lyra to talk to; otherwise, explanation takes time and gets in the way. So I had a man come through the door with a gun.

Mark Lawson: Thank you very much. I believe there's going to be a book signing now. Only two books each, please.

Philip Pullman: Yes, and could the children be allowed to go first in the queue?

Postscript by George Beahm: The *Sunday Times* Oxford Literary Festival put on 175 events over six days; 270 speakers spoke to a crowd estimated at 30,000 people. Predictably, the biggest draw was Philip Pullman, who, reported the *Times,* was mobbed by book dealers, prompting the besieged author to set priorities. "You have to let the real readers to the front of the queue," he said.

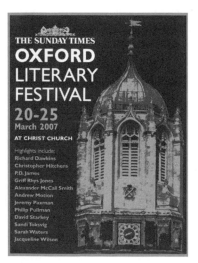

A booklet for the Sunday Times *Oxford Literary Festival, featuring Philip Pullman*

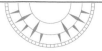

Film Quips from All Over: On Casting, Crew, and the Movie

PRODUCER **Deborah Forte** on the long road from book to film: "This project started for me almost eleven years ago when I read the manuscript for *Northern Lights,* which is the name of *The Golden Compass* in the U.K. When I read the manuscript, I thought to myself, 'Who is this extraordinary writer?' I had never read Philip's work before. And wherever he's going, I want to go with him. And it struck me that this material was singularly visual, emotional, and cinematic. And I called him about making a film and he said, 'Okay, I think it's a good idea. Even though films never get made from books that are options, let's see what happens.' It took a very long time. It's ten years later now and it's been a really interesting journey." (From canmag.com)

COCHAIRMEN/CO-CEOs of New Line Cinema, **Bob Shaye** and **Michael Lynne**: "*The Golden Compass* is the most ambitious film that New Line has undertaken since *The Lord of the Rings* trilogy, and we have assembled a remarkable creative team, headed by Chris Weitz, to bring it to fruition." (From a New Line Cinema press release, June 29, 2006)

AUTHOR **Philip Pullman**, on the casting of Nicole Kidman as Mrs. Coulter: "I always hoped she would play Mrs. Coulter because of all the wonderful qualities she has as an actress." (*Oxford Mail,* Aug. 16, 2006)

PRODUCTION DESIGNER **Dennis Gassner**, on putting together the world of *The Golden Compass*: "The question that I had for everybody was: What is *The Golden Compass*? And to me, I deal in symbols,

I'm the architect of the film. How do you get into a world like this which is a very unusual world, one that I haven't created and nobody has? So you start with that, something simple. The simplicity for me was actually the sphere which became the golden compass. The symbol for purity for Lyra and then the antithesis of that would be for me the oval, and you can start to build the world from there." (From Rebecca Murray, "Behind the Scenes of *The Golden Compass* with Dennis Gassner," http://movies.about.com)

COSTUME DESIGNER **Ruth Myers**, on the extensive costuming involved: "My department has made something like 600 costumes. We've painted, we've manufactured, we've done all sorts of extraordinary things. We've taken modern things and played with them. We made period things; we moved them around. . . . Mrs. Coulter, I wanted to essentially give you the sense of being the most glamorous woman in the world, but I didn't want it to be loud glamour." (From Rebecca Murray, "Costume Designer Ruth Myers Discusses *The Golden Compass*," http://movies.about.com)

CHILD ACTRESS **Dakota Blue Richards**, on her role as Lyra Belacqua: "I feel I can relate to her. I like to think I'm quite brave. I stand up for myself. And I don't let other people tell me what to do. Well, unless it's my mum." (Devin Gordon, "The Arctic Adventurer," *Newsweek,* Dec. 25, 2006)

WRITER-DIRECTOR **Chris Weitz**, on the difficult casting of Lyra, picked from the 10,000 girls who auditioned: "Usually, it's a gut-wrenching decision. You realize the whole time how much rests on the shoulders of this kid. But I didn't have any doubts about Dakota. She looks not quite tamed, and that's Lyra. It was hard to cast someone, honestly, because you may be doing them a disservice. I don't know if anyone can prepare Dakota for the kind of exposure that's going to come with this. Especially in England, where the press can be merciless." (Devin Gordon, "The Arctic Adventurer," *Newsweek,* Dec. 25, 2006)

AUTHOR **Philip Pullman** on the casting of Dakota Blue Richards as Lyra: "I'm delighted with the casting of Dakota Blue Richards as Lyra. As soon as I saw Dakota's screen test, I realized that the search was over. Dakota has just the combination of qualities that make up the complicated character of this girl, and I very much look forward to seeing the film take shape, with Dakota's Lyra at the heart of it." (New Line Cinema press release, "New Line Cinema Greenlights *The Golden Compass* for a September 4 Start Date," June 28, 2006)

ACTOR **Daniel Craig** (Lord Asriel) on *The Golden Compass*: "I was in Rome promoting Bond the other day and we got asked quite a few questions about *The Golden Compass*. The thing is, having spoken to Philip Pullman now at length—he's such a passionate, great guy—there's nothing antireligious about this film. It's antiestablishment in a big way and antitotalitarian and anticontrolling. But essentially it's a film about growing up, and how difficult that can be."

ACTRESS **Eva Green** (Serafina Pekkala) on her role: "I read the Philip Pullman trilogy and really liked the role. She's strong and hundreds of years old. She is a witch who is a guide, philosopher, and friend to Lyra. It is quite a mysterious role which I found attractive. . . . I wanted to make her sound quite otherworldly and yet from another age. I worked with my voice coach, Roison Carty, to create a sort of medieval Scandinavian drawl." (From www.empireonline.com)

AUTHOR **Philip Pullman** on Sam Elliot (Lee Scoresby): "Sam's resemblance to the Lee in my mind is just astonishing. His Lee has all the presence, the experience, the battered integrity, the humor, and the courage of the aeronaut who first walked into my story thirteen years ago. I can't imagine a better cast, and the sets and costumes are just astounding." (From www.philip-pullman.com)

CHRISTIAN NEWSLETTER EDITOR **Simon Jenkins**: "I'm sure this new film will launch 100 anti-film and anti-book websites going through all the detailed reasons why they are wrong and why they are dangerous and pose a threat to civilisation as we know it. But that's not my view of it. I think that is counterproductive. I think it's better to engage with the books on all the issues." (From www.christianitytoday.com)

AIN'T IT COOL WEST COAST CORRESPONDENT **Drew McWeeny** ("Moriarty") after visiting the set of *The Golden Compass*: "I'm just not sure I believe this is going to be New Line's new *Lord of the Rings*, which it needs to be based on the amount of money the studio is putting into the first film, *The Golden Compass*. . . . But can $150 million buy you an audience? . . . This is a huge, crazy challenge. My suggestion is this: 'Lyra is special. Here's the alethiometer that she uses. It tells her what to do. Here's her dæmon shifting shapes. It helps her. They're on a journey. Where? North! Why? Save some kids! Polar bear! Daniel Craig! Cowboy! Lyra in the machine in danger! Nicole Kidman! TITLE UP. And then pray. It's your best bet." (From www.aintitcool.com)

AUTHOR **Philip Pullman**: "So it's possible to say already, at this early stage, that the film will look spectacular, that the cast is superb, and that it sticks pretty closely to my story. What more could I ask for? Maybe a walk-on part; but I don't want to spoil it. I'm greatly looking forward to the premiere." (From www.timesonline.co.uk)

Steamer

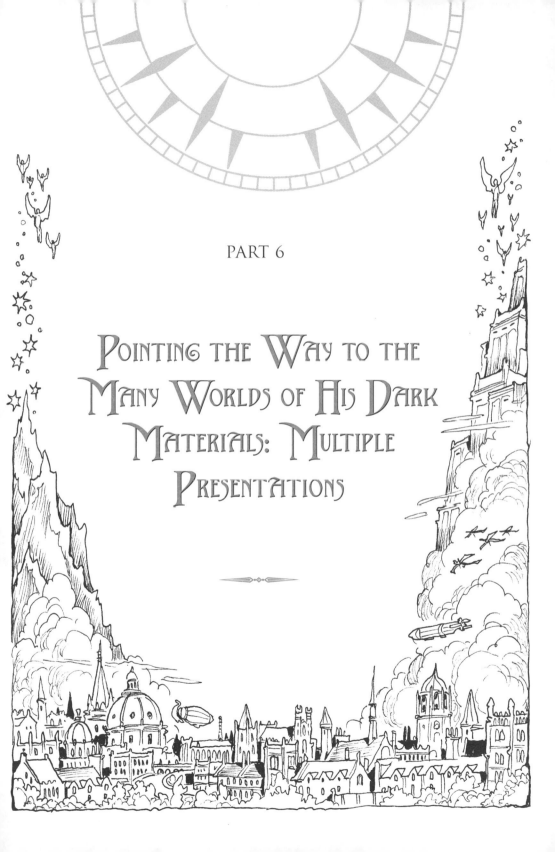

PART 6

Pointing the Way to the Many Worlds of His Dark Materials: Multiple Presentations

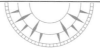

The Theatre Adaptation
of His Dark Materials

I DON'T THINK ANYTHING IS IMPOSSIBLE IN THE
THEATRE. BUT IT IS GOING TO BE TERRIBLY DIFFICULT.
—Pullman, on mounting the play, quoted in *Darkness Illuminated*

I COULD BE WRONG ABOUT THE WHOLE THING. IT
MIGHT SIMPLY NOT WORK.
—Director Nicholas Hytner, quoted in *Darkness Illuminated*

n *The Letters of J. R. R. Tolkien,* he specifically pointed out his desire that *The Lord of the Rings* serve as a source of inspiration to other creators—artists, musicians, and dramatists. Given its broad canvas, it's no wonder that over a half century after its original appearance, Tolkien's seminal work of fantasy has continued to inspire writers, poets, artists (in multiple media), musicians, sculptors, and thespians who apply their unique talents to interpretations of Middle-earth.

Similarly, His Dark Materials has inspired countless fans and pros alike to interpret Lyra's world—most notably, the ambitious effort to bring it to the stage.

On January 3, 2004, the National Theatre in England premiered *His Dark Materials,* a two-part play that, with twenty-minute breaks between acts, ran twelve hours over two days. Requiring a large cast (thirty people), extensive puppetry for the many dæmons and animals, and a drum-revolve stage that allowed quick setups and transitions, *His Dark Materials* obviously faced numerous logistic and creative challenges, not the least of which was the requirement to compress a lengthy story to its essence. The key, Pullman wrote in his introduction to *Philip Pullman's HIS DARK MATERIALS* (Heinemann Plays), was to focus on its central character:

> It was very important that any adaptation should put this little girl, whom I later came to know as Lyra, right at the heart of the story. . . . How could it ever be made to work on the stage? Well, the answer, as Nicholas Wright discovered when he wrote this brilliant adaptation, is to keep Lyra and her quest in mind from the very beginning. Everything else—the dæmons, the huge conflicts, the strange adventures in stranger worlds— all falls into place once that central truth is understood.

Not surprisingly, reviews from theatre critics in the leading U.K. newspapers ran the gamut from faint to loud praise, but the fact remains that public demand required two separate productions with different casts. The result? In the words of a reviewer for BBC *Newsround,* "It's a stunning show" and "This is a great introduction to the books if you don't know them. If you're already a Pullman fan, you won't be disappointed!"

BOOKS

Unfortunately, there are no videotaped recordings of the play available; however, several books capture the story behind the mounting of this production, including publishing the theatre script.

> *His Dark Materials: Based on the Novels by Philip Pullman, Adapted by Nicholas Wright.* The program (or playbill) of the production that opened on December 8, 2004. Measuring 5.5 x 9.5 inches and predominantly printed on heavy stock in two colors (black and red), the playbill provides a detailed listing of its cast and crew credits, the show poster, literary quotes, medieval woodcut reproductions, selected photos, an interview with Pullman conducted by Robert Butler (reprinted from *Darkness Illuminated*), an interview with Nicholas Wright, who adapted the play (reprinted from *Darkness Illuminated*), a nonfiction piece by Pullman (a letter from the angel Xaphania to Lord Asriel on the subject of the Gallivespians), an abbreviated glossary of things, places, people, and other beings in His Dark Materials, and a second nonfiction piece by Pullman (an extract from

"History of the Magisterium," an article in the *Encyclopaedia Europaica*).

Darkness Illuminated: Platform Discussions on "His Dark Materials" at the National Theatre. Measuring 4.5 x 7 inches, with distinctive black printing on black cover stock, this is a book of interviews with Nicholas Hytner (the director), Philip Pullman (two interviews with the author), Nicholas Wright (the adapter), Rowan Williams (Archbishop of Canterbury), two actors (Anna Maxwell Martin who played Lyra, and Dominic Cooper who played Will), and four members of the production crew.

The Art of Darkness: Staging the Philip Pullman Trilogy, by Robert Butler, a drama critic for the newspaper, *Independent on Sunday.* Measuring 6.5 x 9.5 inches, this book is, according to its back cover copy, an "intimate backstage account" that "takes us into the meetings, workshops and rehearsals where, over six months, Pullman's 1300-page novel—about dæmons, armoured bears and parallel universes—was transformed into six hours of drama." Profusely illustrated with photographs of the principals, this book is an authoritative look at how the production was mounted, from its conception to successful conclusion.

Philip Pullman's HIS DARK MATERIALS: Based on the Novels by Philip Pullman, Adapted by Nicholas Wright. Paper-on-board, this book measures 5.25 inches by 8 inches. With introductions by Philip Pullman and Nicholas Wright, illustrated with photos from the production itself, this is the full text of the play as written by Nicholas Wright.

Philip Pullman's HIS DARK MATERIALS: Based on the novels by Philip Pullman, Adapted by Nicholas Wright. This book reprints Wright's theatre script, with a new introduction by Wright.

Supplementary Products

Sold at the National Theatre gift shop and via its online store, the tie-in products are out of stock.

143

A **T-shirt,** black, with silver stamping of an angel with Pullman's signature printed on the right side of the image.

A coffee/tea **mug.** It uses heat-sensitive inks so that, when you pour a hot liquid into it, an image magically appears—hence its title, a "Magic Mug." Stamped in three colors: Pullman's name in white, and "His Dark/Materials/NT" in purple and puce. The mug itself is black.

A **magicube.** Measuring approximately three inches square, the cube is printed with full color designs on all sides, each comprised of four small squares: an angel image, Will and Lyra under a tree (two sides of the cube), the Golden Monkey puppet, the profiles of two puppets with text ("Heads

A photograph of the hornbeam trees, in an expanded view of the cube manufactured for the National Theatre

in one world, tails in another"), and an image of the moon with text ("I spread my wings and brush ten million other worlds"). When opened, eight-square images are revealed: a landscape view of the hornbeam trees in Oxford, Cittàgazze (with text: "There are as many worlds as there are possibilities"), and a map of Lyra's Oxford (from the puzzle design).

"The Alethiometer," a small **brochure** that folds to four by six inches. When opened, it provides information on "The history of the Alethiometer" and instructions, "How to read the Alethiometer." On its reverse side, a large color drawing, a close-up, of an alethiometer with explanatory text as to its symbols and meanings; beneath the illustration, an explanation of its symbology.

A **puzzle** of Lyra's Oxford. The puzzle itself measures eleven by fifteen inches, and is printed in

A pamphlet about the alethiometer, published by the National Theatre

three colors: black, light blue, and beige; the wooden frame
encasing the puzzle is one inch in width. According to the
staff at the National Theatre Bookshop, this was issued in a
limited edition of only 150 puzzles. According to its liner
notes, this is "a wooden Windsor puzzle in a frame, laser
cut into 280 challenging pieces, intended for advance
puzzlers. Size 385 by 282 mm. Produced exclusively for the
National Theatre Bookshop by Robert Longstaff
Workshops with permission." The puzzle comes with a
two-part stand.

*Close-up of an
angel for a T-shirt
designed for the
National Theatre*

*A black-colored mug with the logo
of the National Theatre on it; when
hot liquid is poured in, an image of
the angel appears on the backside.*

*"Heads in one world, tails in
another." A quotation from His
Dark Materials printed on the
cube manufactured for the
National Theatre*

NT

The Art of Darkness

Staging the Philip Pullman trilogy

by Robert Butler

The Good, the Bad, and the Ugly: Reviews of the Play by British Newspapers

he following reviews of the stage version of *His Dark Materials* were reported by BBC News in January 2004.

Times: "I must admit that, lover of all things bold and imaginative though I hope I am, I was weary by the end. I had had my fill of rushing witches, men waving bear masks, screeching harpies, the camp-sounding mannequins who trail white taffeta and claim to be angels, the lizard-headed flying nightgowns known as cliff-ghasts, the cute dolls in period costumes that ride on large green flies, and even the mammals, birds or reptiles which are carried by actors or manipulated by puppeteers in order to represent characters' spirits or 'dæmons.' And I had had more than my fill of Pullman's mind."

Independent: "It wasn't the parts where the Olivier Theatre was showing off its astonishing resources (with the mighty drum-revolve working overtime to dredge up diverse worlds) that made the keenest impact on me. The bits that I shall treasure are the moments of heart-stopping simplicity where Wright, Hytner and the two superb central performers (Anna Maxwell Martin and Dominic Cooper) prove they have grasped the emotional core of this inspiring saga, a colossally arduous rite of passage into puberty in which a pair of twelve-year-olds from parallel universes redemptively re-enact the Fall, their positive embrace of sexual love and adult consciousness liberating Creation from the life-denying repression of the wicked Christian church."

Daily Mail: "For all its extravagance and scope, with a huge drum-like set heaving into view while the periphery revolves in the changing landscape of mountains, snow bridges and encampments, this is a distinctly stop-go affair. Fluency and magic are in short supply both in a rather pedestrian script by Nicholas Wright and the faltering dramatic momentum of Nicholas Hytner's production. Partly this is due to the books themselves. Whatever their merits (and I'm not convinced), they are not Charles Dickens or Victor Hugo."

Guardian: "Nothing is more tempting than the apparently impossible. But, although director Nicholas Hytner and his creative team display heroic courage in turning Philip Pullman's epic trilogy into two three-hour plays, they are ultimately overcome by the vastness of the enterprise. There is much to admire in the staging; yet the result, inevitably, is like a clipped hedge compared to Pullman's forest."

Daily Telegraph: "The stage version of His Dark Materials strikes me as an honourable failure rather than an exhilarating success. There are some striking moments and several superb performances, but too often the production seems earthbound when it ought to soar, depressingly literal when it ought to fire the imagination. Whisper it ever so quietly, but there were long stretches when I was bored."

Observer: "Dæmons, cliff-ghasts, lovelorn witches, Gyptians, harpies, armoured bears, soul-sucking spectres and tiny creatures riding dragonflies—the magical creations of writer Philip Pullman soared from page to stage yesterday in what could be the most spectacular theatre blockbuster ever. One of Pullman's best-loved but trickiest inventions, the dæmons—devoted animals that are a physical manifestation of a person's soul—become paper puppets illuminated by an internal light and controlled by masked operators dressed in black so the audience almost forgets their presence. His armoured bear—warrior polar bears— are suggested by costumes and masks held forward by the actors in a technique reminiscent of the stage version of *The Lion King*."

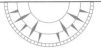

The Radio Dramatization Originally Broadcast on the BBC

BBC Audiobooks

Northern Lights was first broadcast on BBC Radio 4 on January 4, 2003. Recorded at BBC Studios. Music composed and performed by Billy Cowie. Produced by David Hunter. Dramatised by Lavinia Murray.

The Subtle Knife was first broadcast on BBC Radio 4 on January 11, 2003. Recorded at BBC Studios. Music composed and performed by Billy Cowie. Produced by Janet Whitaker. Dramatised by Lavinia Murray.

The Amber Spyglass was first broadcast on BBC Radio 4 on January 18, 2003. Recorded at BBC Studios. Music composed and performed by Billie Cowie. Produced by David Hunter. Dramatised by Lavinia Murray.

Devout Sceptics (the interview with Pullman on the bonus CD) was first broadcast on BBC Radio 4, August 9, 2001. Produced by Malcolm Love. From the liner notes: "In this series Bel Mooney interviewed a prominent person each week. Each believes that the big ideas concerning God, religion and spirituality are very important, but are unconvinced by traditional explanations."

A boxed set of seven CDs: two for each book, and one for *His Dark Materials* (the interview with Pullman), packaged with four mini-posters. Running time of eight hours. (The CDs are available separately by book, but the CD with the Pullman interview, which runs 27.6 minutes, is not.)

The dramatization of His Dark Materials, broadcast on the BBC

The closest thing to a stage presentation, this dramatization bridges the gap between the stage presentation and the unabridged reading of the book. Its advantage and, ironically, its disadvantage is that the necessity for compression, to make the book to a manageable length, means cuts in subject matter were made, and some of Pullman's carefully chosen words are changed or discarded. (Notably: In the books, the Golden Monkey, the dæmon for Mrs. Coulter, is never named. But in this dramatization, the dæmon is named Ozymandias, after Percy Bysshe Shelley's 1818 sonnet.)

The matter of Pullman's exquisitely crafted prose being changed is the dramatization's most obvious drawback. Speaking at the Oxford Literary Festival in 2007 about the similar, necessary changes made to his books to adapt them to the screen, Pullman lamented the loss of "all my beautiful prose!" For a writer like Pullman who chooses his words *very* carefully, a poorly done dramatization can change the "taste" of the prose: Tokay becomes water, saffron becomes salt. In this case, the job done is serviceable but not inspired, which is why I prefer the original text in any form to the best adaptation in any other form.

UNABRIDGED AUDIO RECORDINGS

Northern Lights. The Subtle Knife. The Amber Spyglass. Twelve compact discs with a running time of fourteen hours, fifty-four minutes.

There is a directness and immediacy to a faithful, unabridged audio recording of a book that makes it in some ways better than a reading of the primary text—*if* the reader is careful and deliberate in his reading. Thankfully, the reader for the unabridged recordings is Pullman himself, who takes exquisite care in reading his text, just as he did in writing it. The result is a listening experience that underscores Pullman's own convictions about storytelling having its roots in the oral, not written, tradition. As Kate Kellaway explained in an interview with Pullman (*Observer,* Oct. 22, 2000):

> Curiously, he describes himself as if he were not a writer either, but part of an oral tradition. He compares himself to a busking storyteller "sitting on a carpet in a market place." He likes to imagine people coming to "sample" his stories. Those who enjoy them "can stay and put coins in the hat." He believes in the storyteller's power.

What makes this audio recording of His Dark Materials so compelling is that although Pullman is the principal reader, he's backed up by a full cast, which provides the voices of the characters, including the dæmons. The result is a delightful audio experience that perfectly captures this lengthy story with all its nuances.

The covers to the unabridged recordings of **The Golden Compass** *and* **The Amber Spyglass** *from Random House Audio Publishing Group*

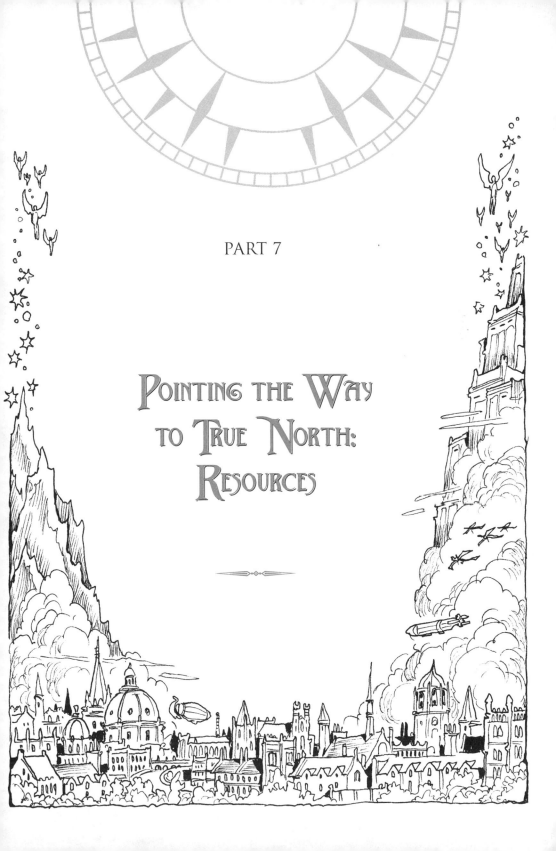

PART 7

POINTING THE WAY
TO TRUE NORTH:
RESOURCES

Philip Pullman Websites

Official Sites

The Official Philip Pullman Website

WWW.PHILIP-PULLMAN.COM
Updates: Infrequent
Plug-ins: none

For Pullman readers, this is obviously the first place to go for information about his life and work. Though Pullman updates his website, he understandably does so on an infrequent basis because writing *The Book of Dust* takes precedence.

Free of the usual bells and whistles, this site doesn't require plug-ins. In terms of design, the green background for all the pages is very easy on the eyes, but the reverse lettering (white on green) is less so.

Two navigational bars allow easy access to all pages on this site. On the left, news-related topics: The Film (referring to the New Line Cinema adaptation of *The Golden Compass*), Theatre (play adaptations), and a news archive.

The navigational bar at the top provides background information about the books (His Dark Materials and other works), about the writing, about the worlds, and about the author, which is extensive. A long, informative autobiographical essay is included ("I have a feeling this all belongs to me," reprinted in this book; see pages 9–33), as are Essays & Articles (links to published pieces, many from the *Guardian* newspaper, to which he's a frequent contributor), Interviews (links to online interviews), and contact information for his agent and publishers, though no e-mail links are provided.

On the far right are links to: His Dark Materials, with text extracts and illustrations by Pullman; *Lyra's Oxford,* with an explanation about where it fits in the cycle of the His Dark Materials stories; Theatre, with information about ongoing projects and book collections; an extensive FAQ section, with very detailed information; and Illustrations, which provides the chapter head art for *Northern Lights* (*The Golden Compass* in the U.S.) and *The Subtle Knife,* but not *The Amber Spyglass.*

Any newcomer to Pullman's works will find a wealth of information on this site that will cover all the major areas of interest in his life and work.

For those seeking current news, especially about the ongoing film adaptations of His Dark Materials, Pullman recommends two fan websites: www.hisdarkmaterials.org and www.bridgetothestars.net.

THE OFFICIAL MOVIE SITE

WWW.GOLDENCOMPASSMOVIE.COM
Updates: Infrequent
Plug-ins: extensive

When you get to the home page, music rises up and you're prompted to choose your language. Once you do so, it takes you to a page that explains Lyra's World. A narrator reads the first paragraph; a scroll bar allows you to read more at your leisure.

The uncredited conceptual art is excellent and suggestive: A red-haired Lyra, with Pan on her shoulder, is watching a male figure, followed by a leopard, walking away from her and toward a distant cityscape.

On the right side, a gold-colored navigational device with an arrow pointing to the right glows, drawing your attention. Clicking on it takes you to pages that tell you about the main characters and organizations, illustrated with photos from the film and concept art that whets the appetite for more.

The second navigation bar takes you to a page showing an interactive alethiometer. "Drag the three red needles to lie over appropriate symbols on the face of the Alethiometer while forming a question in your mind. Click the '?' button and the fourth needle will respond, swinging over different symbols to form an answer."

Don't be disappointed if you can't understand what the alethiometer is trying to tell you. Lyra, after all, was a natural at it, but it takes (as any Pullman reader knows) years of hard work to attain competency in reading this truth-measuring device.

The last window, "About the Film," provides updates and stills from the movie, and a listing of its cast and crew.

With two more films in the series, the domains for subtleknifemovie.com and amberspyglassmovie.com have already been registered.

THE OFFICIAL U.S. BOOK SITE

Philip Pullman: His Dark Materials

WWW.HISDARKMATERIALS.COM
redirects to: www.randomhouse.com/features/pullman

The colorful, elegantly designed trade paperback editions of His Dark Materials are highlighted, along with the deluxe edition (tenth anniversary) of *The Golden Compass.*

This site is geared toward booksellers and the media, and not the general reader. It offers general information about the books, the author, how to read the alethiometer, an e-mailed newsletter about fantasy authors, and a downloadable podcast of an interview conducted with Pullman, Christopher Paolini, and Tamora Pierce.

UNOFFICIAL FAN SITES

WWW.HISDARKMATERIALS.ORG

Fans of His Dark Materials will love this site because if there's anything you can think of about those books, it's answered here: With extensive coverage about each book, the movie adaptation, books about Pullman, audiobooks, and radio dramatizations, this site explores every aspect of His Dark Materials.

It also hosts a message board, a chat room, an encyclopedia, a role-playing game, and photographs.

Well-designed and interactive, this site is a "must" for any Pullman

157

fan. It's easy to spend hours getting lost in the worlds of His Dark Materials through this site.

For fun, check out your dæmon name generator. Choose the sex of the dæmon and click on "Tell me my Dæmon's name!" Highly recommended.

WWW.BRIDGETOTHESTARS.NET

Less elaborate in design than its counterpart, this is nonetheless an excellent site with extensive coverage about His Dark Materials, especially news, which is the principal attraction of the home page.

The site covers His Dark Materials, *Lyra's Oxford,* news about *The Book of Dust,* the movie and stage adaptation, and other adaptations, as well.

Resources include an encyclopedia, photographs provided by fans, information about the science of His Dark Materials, books about Pullman, web links to fan-generated essays and columns, and a useful section about how His Dark Materials can be taught in classrooms.

Fans will love the message board, the interactive section (chat room, AIM icons, wallpapers, and quizzes), fan art, and fan fiction. Highly recommended.

OTHER SITES OF INTEREST

WWW.EXETER.OX.AC.UK/COLLEGE/

Exeter College: University of Oxford

His Dark Materials readers will recognize this as the real-world model for Pullman's fictional Jordan College. Pullman, an Honorary Fellow of the College, read English here and graduated in 1968.

Another one of its "Old Members" (Exeter's term for alumni) was J. R. R. Tolkien, who was "an undergraduate at Exeter College. He was not just author of *The Hobbit* and *The Lord of the Rings*, but also one of the foremost philologists and Old English scholars of the century."

Though this site is geared toward prospective students, it's a good place to visit to get a sense of this small but important college in the Oxford University system.

WWW.EBAY.COM

Online auction site.

In the course of researching this book, I checked eBay on a daily basis, looking for inexpensive reading copies, limited editions, signed items, and the rare and unusual. In all cases, ebay.com delivered. In fact, the only item I wanted to buy but didn't was a limited edition hardback book of 1000 copies, given to cast and crew members. When the first copy of *The Golden Compass Cast and Crew Journal* appeared on eBay, just days after Pullman's 2007 appearance at the Oxford Literary Festival, the fevered bidding ended at an astonishing $885.33! An exceptional item at an exceptional price, more copies will likely surface.

WWW.ADDALL.COM

New and used books.

Here's how effective this website is when searching for an impossible-to-find book: In the past I've used, with great results, www.abebooks.com, which searches booksellers worldwide for the rare and the obscure, but even that failed to turn up a copy of Connie Kirk's *J. K. Rowling Encyclopedia,* a book that mysteriously went out of print soon after its publication. (Even a query to its author proved fruitless.) No matter. After finding out about www.addall.com and clicking on "used books," I was able to choose among four offered copies.

Though amazon.com is useful for forthcoming and in-print books, I find www.addall.com indispensable for locating the elusive but necessary title that, because it canvasses over two dozen sites, can consolidate them all into one search. An indispensable resource.

Anbaric Park

KEY FILM COLLECTIBLES

he *Golden Compass Cast and Crew Journal*, in hardback, 155 pages, published by New Line Cinema, in an edition of 1,000. Given out to principals, this is not available to the public. The book has photos taken on set, conceptual art, models, and candid photos.

The Golden Compass pressbook, in paperback, 16 pages, of which 12 are on coated posterboard stock and 4 are on lighter stock. Published by New Line Cinema, edition size unknown. An oversized, full-color publication measuring 12 x 17 inches, the front and back covers feature golden rings surrounded by symbology.

The book includes: a translucent sheet with an image of the stylized film title, seen through the front cover; the alethiometer; text introducing the movie, superimposed against a skyline of Oxford spread over two pages; two pages devoted to Dakota Blue Richards as Lyra Belacqua; two pages devoted to Nicole Kidman as Mrs. Coulter; two pages devoted to Daniel Craig as Lord Asriel; biographies of principals behind and in front of the camera; "The World of *The Golden Compass*," listing and discussing key characters in the film; and an image of Iorek Byrnison in body armor, which is reversed for the last page, so it can be seen through the die-cut window on the back cover.

Usually available for approximately $30 on eBay.

BOOK EDITIONS OF HIS DARK MATERIALS

THE GOLDEN COMPASS
(in the United Kingdom, *Northern Lights*)

1. **The Deluxe 10th Anniversary Edition.** Knopf. Trade hardback with dust jacket, $22.95. This is the edition of choice, not only because of its excellent production values, but because it includes "some papers from the Library of Jordan College" whose authorship is Lord Asriel. A handsome book with a matching, embossed dust jacket and a gold-colored silk ribbon, this is the first of three in a matching set.

2. **The signed, limited edition.** Scholastic UK. Published in 2005 under its original title, *Northern Lights*, this had a retail price of £30. Bound in blue cloth with matching dust jacket, illustrated endpapers, and an illustrated slipcase, this edition includes "Notes by Lord Asriel from Jordan College Library" (subsequently reprinted in Knopf's deluxe tenth anniversary edition). This is a limited edition of 1000 copies, numbered and signed by Philip Pullman. (Note: This is out of print and, when sold as a set with its matching two books, sells for up to $756 on the secondary market; see www.abebooks.com or www.ebay.com.)

3. **Trade hardback.** Knopf. Trade hardback with dust jacket, $20. This is the original edition, with jacket art by Eric Rohmann.

4. **Trade paperback.** Knopf. Trade paperback, $11.95. This features an imaginative zodiac design by Ericka Meltzer O'Rourke and title lettering by Lilly Lee.

5. **Unabridged CD.** From Knopf, $44. An unabridged reading by Philip Pullman, with a full cast that brings the individual characters to life with their distinctive voices. The nine compact discs run ten hours, forty-nine minutes.

6. **BBC Dramatization.** *His Dark Materials.* £36. Available from

www.amazon.co.uk, this is packaged along with recordings of *The Subtle Knife* and *The Amber Spyglass* in a handsome boxed set with liner notes. Included in this set, a short interview conducted with Pullman by the BBC.

One of four mini-posters folded as an insertion in the boxed set of the BBC dramatization of His Dark Materials

THE SUBTLE KNIFE

1. **The Deluxe 10th Anniversary Edition.** Knopf. Trade hardback with dust jacket, $22.99. Designed to match the deluxe tenth anniversary edition of *The Golden Compass,* the production values are similarly impressive. The appendices include notes and drawings by Colonel John Parry.

2. **The signed, limited edition.** Scholastic U.K. Published in 2005, this had a retail price of £30. Bound in red cloth with matching dust jacket, illustrated endpapers, and an illustrated slipcase, this edition includes "notes and drawings by Colonel John Parry" (subsequently reprinted in Knopf's deluxe tenth anniversary edition). This is a limited edition of 1000 copies, numbered and signed by Philip Pullman. Out of print.

3. **Trade hardback.** Knopf. Trade hardback with dust jacket, $20. This is the original edition, with jacket art by Eric Rohmann.

4. **Trade paperback.** Knopf. Trade paperback, $11.95. This features an imaginative zodiac design by Ericka Meltzer O'Rourke and title lettering by Lilly Lee.

5. **Unabridged CD.** From Knopf, $40. An unabridged reading by Philip Pullman, with a full cast that brings the individual characters to life with their distinctive voices. The eight compact discs run eight hours, fifty-five minutes. (Note: The newer edition, issued by Listening Library for $44, reflects the packaging of the anniversary Knopf editions.)

THE AMBER SPYGLASS

1. **The Deluxe 10th Anniversary Edition.** Knopf. Trade hardback with dust jacket, $22.99. As with the two previous volumes, this is elegantly designed and features papers by Mary Malone from Secret Magisterium Files.

2. **The signed, limited edition.** Scholastic U.K. Published in 2005, this had a retail price of £30. Bound in gold-colored cloth with matching dust jacket, illustrated endpapers, and an illustrated slipcase, this edition includes papers by Mary Malone from Secret Magisterium Files. This is a limited edition of 1000 copies, numbered and signed by Philip Pullman. Out of print.

3. **Trade hardback.** Knopf. Trade hardback with dust jacket, $19.95. This features the art of Eric Rohmann.

4. **Trade paperback.** Knopf. Trade paperback, $11.95. This features an imaginative zodiac design by Ericka Meltzer O'Rourke and title lettering by Lilly Lee.

5. **Unabridged CD.** From Knopf, $54. An unabridged reading by Philip Pullman, with a full cast that brings the individual characters to life with their distinctive voices. The twelve compact discs run fourteen hours, fifty-four minutes.

An angel and the Golden Monkey on a four-square cube, manufactured for the National Theatre production of His Dark Materials

Books About Philip Pullman and His Work

BookValuer: Philip Pullman, by bookvaluer.com (no place of publication or publication date given). A useful, 16-page pamphlet that provides an autobiographical profile of Pullman, a detailed bibliography of his work (first editions and other important editions), valuations, and buying tips. Recommended especially for the investor or for insurance purposes for collection valuation.

Dark Matter: Shedding Light on Philip Pullman's His Dark Materials, by Tony Watkins. InterVarsity Press, 2004. The reader should know that InterVarsity Press is the book publishing division of InterVarsity Christian Fellowship/USA, "a student movement active on campus at hundreds of universities, colleges and schools of nursing . . . and a member movement of the International Fellowship of Evangelical Students." In the preface, Mr. Watkins writes: "I do not assume or expect that you share my own Christian perspectives, but I do believe that it's helpful for all fans of Pullman's works—Christian or otherwise—to *understand* a Christian perspective on it. That does not mean there is an obviously Christian angle right through this book, or that it is consistently negative." That said, his book seems balanced in its approach. I didn't feel as if Mr. Watkins was attempting to beat me repeatedly over my head with his Christian viewpoints, and I don't think you'll feel that way, either. In other words, keep an open mind and give this book a try. You might be surprised at what you'll discover.

Dark Matters: An Unofficial and Unauthorised Guide to Philip Pullman's Internationally Bestselling His Dark Materials Trilogy, by Lance Parkin and Mark Jones. Virgin Books, 2005. Divided into four parts, the bulk of the book is an alphabetical listing of the people, places, and things in His Dark Materials. Other material includes a brief biography about Pullman culled from public domain sources, and a detailed look at His Dark Materials, *Lyra's Oxford,* and *The Book of Dust.*

Darkness Visible: Inside the World of Philip Pullman, by Nicholas Tucker. ibooks, 2003. Written with Pullman's participation, it is a good overview of Pullman's books. Tucker (a former teacher and educational psychologist, currently a senior lecturer at the University of Sussex) provides an excellent biography and covers the Sally Lockhart novels and other works, but devotes most of the space to His Dark Materials.

The Devil's Account: Philip Pullman & Christianity, by Hugh Rayment-Pickard. Darton, Longman and Todd, 2004. A parish priest with a PhD in philosophy of religion, Rayment-Pickard points out a salient fact: that Pullman, whose personal viewpoint is that of an atheist, spends an inordinate amount of time in his novels postulating theological conundrums—but why? "I became even more curious about the nature of Pullman's religious concerns: was he simply hostile to religion, or was there perhaps a religious quest hidden somewhere within his antagonism?" This book attempts to answer that question, without using a sledgehammer to drive the point home. A thoughtful and illuminating book that concludes, "Everyone likes straightforward answers to straightforward questions. But given the paradoxes at the heart of Pullman's writing, straightforward answers may not be forthcoming. Pullman's writing may be the kind that supplies more questions than answers." To which I say: amen.

The Elements of His Dark Materials: A Guide to Philip Pullman's Trilogy, by Laurie Frost; foreword by Philip Pullman. Fell Press, 2006. This 542-page encyclopedia is from a small press. As Pullman notes in his foreword to the book, it is indispensable for anyone with more than a casual interest in His Dark Materials. It is an outstanding, and eminently useful, work of scholarship. It's divided into sections and sports a reference section as well: characters; places and peoples; creatures, beings, and extraordinary humans; the alethiometer, the Subtle Knife, the Amber Spyglass; Philosophy, Psychology, and Theology; Applied Metaphysics; Applied Sciences and Technology; The Natural Sciences; Social Structures of the Worlds; Languages and Diction; Allusions; Epigraphs; and a bibliography, His Dark Materials references, and works cited. This book earns my highest recommendation and I could sing its praises until I'm hoarse, but I think Pullman should have the last word here: "I can't recommend it too highly to the reader who's found anything interesting or enjoyable in this story of mine. . . . It's flattering, of course, to find one's work the object of such care and attention; but how much more satisfying when the work of reference that results is so accurate, and so interesting, and so full."

Exploring Philip Pullman's His Dark Materials, by Lois H. Gresh. St. Martin's Press, 2007. Like me, Lois Gresh writes pop culture books on unauthorized subjects, hence this book's subtitle: "An Unauthorized Adventure through *The Golden Compass, The Subtle Knife,* and *The Amber Spyglass.*" Though the book is, as expected, excellent, its title is somewhat misleading, since readers will likely expect a book exploring His Dark Materials, when in fact this book uses His Dark Materials principally as a point of departure. In her preface, she states, "This book delves into the *subjects* behind His Dark Materials. As such, it is not a book about the story lines and subplots, the characterization, and the writing style in His Dark Materials. Instead, the focus is on angels, souls, the afterlife, Dust, dark matter, and quantum entanglement: the meat of the books." Gresh's principal skill, as exhibited by her many other books, is popularizing science to a general readership, which she does here. But fans looking to read the characters, geography, and worlds found in His Dark Materials will have to look elsewhere.

His Dark Materials Illuminated: Critical Essays on Philip Pullman's Trilogy, edited by Millicent Lenz with Carole Scott. Wayne State University Press, 2005. Fantasy is being taken very seriously in academic circles. One look at the subjects of papers at Harry Potter proceedings is enough to make the point: Fantasy is no longer just kid's stuff. In this anthology, fourteen essays are thematically organized in three sections: Reading fantasy, figuring human nature; intertextuality and revamping traditions; and Pullman and theology, Pullman and science fiction. If you've ever hungered to know about "Pullman's Enigmatic Ontology: Revamping Old Traditions in His Dark Materials" (by Carole Scott, an English professor at San Diego State University), this is where you can find it and its cousins, with similar titles that will excite mostly academicians. Though not light reading, its essays are thought-provoking and delve deeper into the mysteries that comprise His Dark Materials.

Inside His Dark Materials, by Nicholas Tucker. Artsmagic. Profile of Pullman and His Dark Materials. Running time, 124 minutes. "A celebratory tribute to Pullman and his books, scripted by the well-known critic Nicholas Tucker, author of *The Rough Guide to Children's Books* as well as *Darkness Visible: Inside the World of Philip Pullman.* Through him, the company has secured an exclusive interview with Philip Pullman himself as well as contributions from friends, former teachers, and many others fascinated by his work." Interviewees include Enid Jones, who taught him English, and a childhood friend, Merfyn Jones.

169

This contains the only known interview with Pullman available on DVD. (Note: Artsmagic released on Nov. 14, 2006, a DVD titled *The World of Philip Pullman: His Life & Works,* with a running time of forty-nine minutes. This is a truncated version of *Inside His Dark Materials,* featuring the interview with Pullman.)

The Magical Worlds of Philip Pullman: A Treasury of Fascinating Facts, by David Colbert. Berkley Books, 2006. Sporting a wonderful cover by Dan Craig, the strength of the book is Colbert's far-ranging curiosity and talent for researching. Posing speculative questions like "What Makes Iorek Byrnison So Smart?" the book explains the inspirations of His Dark Materials, including Milton's *Paradise Lost,* William Blake, and the Bible. An excellent background introduction to His Dark Materials, especially for students who, as a result, may want to consult the primary texts. On the downside: The cheap newsprint paper stock used inside is a significant departure from the quality offset paper used in Colbert's other books, with the regrettable result that the printing in this book is underwhelming.

Navigating "The Golden Compass": Religion, Science and Dæmonology in Philip Pullman's His Dark Materials, edited by Glenn Yeffeth. BenBella Books, 2005. An anthology of eighteen essays, this is an accessible collection intended for the general reader, bridging the gap to the more academic texts. The best among them: Novelist Michael Chabon's "Dust and Dæmons," which originally appeared in the *New York Review of Books* and is by far the most insightful piece in this collection. (I'm less than thrilled by Kay Kenyon's "Reading by Flashlight: What Fantasy Writers Can Learn from Pullman," in which she attributes Pullman's success to "certain publishing and fictional choices unrelated to the quality of writing," when in fact, as Pullman has patiently explained, it's *all* about the quality of the writing: the plot, the theme, the narrative power, the characterizations, and the use of language.)

Philip Pullman, by Margaret Speaker-Yuan. Part of the "Who Wrote That?" biography series. Chelsea House, 2006. Intended for younger readers and illustrated with photographs, this is a good overview of Pullman's life and career. It doesn't appear that Pullman participated, so it lacks new nuggets of information that are provided in some of the other books.

Philip Pullman's His Dark Materials Trilogy: A Reader's Guide, by Claire Squires. Continuum, 2004. This small book (ninety-five pages) is part of a series called "Continuum Contemporaries." According to the publisher, "The aim of this series is to provide accessible and informative introductions to the most popular, most acclaimed and most influential novels of recent years" using a uniform template: a short biography of the novelist, a full-length study of the novels, a summary of how the novels were received when initially published, a summary of the novels' contemporary standing, discussion questions, suggestions for further reading, and useful websites. I think Squires, who is a senior lecturer in publishing at Oxford Brookes University, did a fine job. I recommend this book to first-timers who want an informative and accurate overview of His Dark Materials before delving deeper into its many mysteries explored by other authors in books like *His Dark Materials Illuminated.*

Philip Pullman: Master of Fantasy, by Susan E. Reichard. Enslow, 2006. A good overview of Pullman's life and work, intended for young readers. The best thing about this book is its exclusive interview conducted in 2004, with the kinds of interesting questions that reporters who haven't read the books wouldn't know enough to ask. For instance, "Can you please discuss the wonderful drawings that you created for each chapter in *The Golden Compass?*" These are informed questions, not the "where do you get your ideas?" kind of question, or "do you believe in God?" I do think—a minor quibble here—that because Pullman is so adamantly against labels in general and the fantasy label in particular that the publisher should change the subtitle to "Master Storyteller."

Philip Pullman, Master Storyteller: A Guide to the Worlds of His Dark Materials, by Claire Squires. The Continuum International Publishing Group, 2006. The strength of this book, as the title makes clear, is that the author emphasizes the storytelling qualities of Pullman. The book itself is a very accessible text that, though clearly criticism, would be a good introduction to a new Pullman fan who wants to know about the storyteller and his most popular work, His Dark Materials. (Pullman's other books are covered, but the emphasis is on the trilogy.) In her closing chapter, Squires rightly concludes that "Philip Pullman has undoubtedly managed to convey an accomplished, captivating, sometimes provocative vision to a legion of readers who have responded imaginatively, whether in excitement, in anger, in appreciation or in wonder. For this, the master storyteller of His Dark Materials has already engaged, and will continue to do so, with millions of readers, provoking them, delighting them and making them think."

The Science of Philip Pullman's His Dark Materials, by Mary and John Gribbin, with an introduction by Philip Pullman. Alfred A. Knopf, 2005. From Pullman's U.S. publisher, this book follows in scope and approach the many books about *Star Trek* and Rowling's novels about Harry Potter—*The Science of Harry Potter: How Magic Really Works, The Physics of Star Trek,* and *The Science of Superheroes,* all of which explore

171

the intersection of fiction and real-world fact. The Gribbins are well-grounded in science, whereas Pullman (as he admits) is "a science fan" and "not fundamentally a scientist." So he applauds their efforts to explain science to a general audience. Like Pullman, I agree that these two are eminently qualified to write about physics; they do so in an entertaining and informative way.

So You Think You Know His Dark Materials? by Clive Gifford. Hodder Children's Books, 2006. More than 1000 questions about Pullman's three novels, with questions organized according to their difficulty: easy, medium, and hard. Examples: "What is the name of the young girl who is in all the books in the His Dark Materials trilogy?" (That's an easy question.) "In which city does Will lose two fingers of his hand?" (That's a medium question.) And "When Lyra finally returns to her own Oxford, whose collection of valuable silver has been looted?" (That's a hard question.) In terms of design, the book is needlessly distracting.

The Wand in the Word: Conversations with Writers of Fantasy, compiled and edited by Leonard S. Marcus. Candlewick Press, 2006. Philip Pullman contributed an interview for this book, illustrated with new photos. In addition to Pullman, other big-name fantasy writers who contributed interviews include Ursula K. Le Guin (Earthsea trilogy), Madeleine L'Engle (the classic *Wrinkle in Time*), Garth Nix, Tamora Pierce, Terry Pratchett, and Jane Yolen—a stellar cast! In terms of book production, this is a beautiful book, as you'd expect from Candlewick Press. The typesetting, paper stock, design, and binding are first-rate. The book's only drawback is its awkward title.

Books about the Play

The Art of Darkness: Staging the Philip Pullman Trilogy, by Robert Butler. National Theatre, 2003. The former drama critic for the *Independent on Sunday,* Mr. Butler has the luxury of having all the room he needs in this book to tell the story about how this ambitious production was staged. In this insider's view, he pulls the curtain back, so to speak, and takes the reader behind the scenes to show how "the meetings, workshops and rehearsals" over a six-month period resulted in the compression of a complex novel into six hours of drama. The book is probably of more interest to drama students than the general reader; the writing is informed and the black-and-white photographs give a sense of what happened onstage as well as off.

Darkness Illuminated: Philip Pullman, Nicholas Hytner, Nicholas Wright, Dr. Rowan Williams & Others on His Dark Materials at the National Theatre, with Robert Butler. Oberon Books, 2004. With black text on a black cover, this small book offers a collection of interviews with all the principals *after* the production was mounted. For this book, interviews were conducted with Nicholas Hytner (the director), David Cauchi (puppet supervisor), Huw Llewellyn (lighting department), Sacha Milroy (production manager), Matt Wilde (staff director), Nicholas Wright (the adapter), two of the actors (Anna Maxwell Martin who plays Lyra, and Dominic Cooper who plays Will), Rowan Williams, and Philip Pullman. The result is a multifaceted, inside look at the production. No photos.

His Dark Materials, based on the novels by Philip Pullman, adapted by Nicholas Wright. National Theatre, 2005. Not paginated. The program book for His Dark Materials. More a printed souvenir of the play than a book proper, it includes a complete list of characters/actors for both shows (Part One, Part Two); an interview with Pullman conducted by Robert Butler; an interview with Nicholas Wright (adapter) conducted by Robert Butler; a letter from Lord Asriel to the angel Xaphania; a short glossary of things, places, people, and other beings, illustrated by Pullman; a fictional extract by Pullman from *History of the Magisterium,* an article in the *Encyclopedia Europaica*; a long quotation by Pullman, published on Amazon.com, about Heinrich von Kleist's essay, "On the Marionette Theatre," which was an influence on His Dark Materials; a "thank you" poem written by a friend of his after *The Amber Spyglass* was published; and detailed credits of the actors and others who worked on this production.

Philip Pullman's His Dark Materials Based on the Novels, adapted by Nicholas Wright. Heinemann, 2005. Sporting brief introductions by Philip Pullman and Nicholas Wright, this publishes the complete screenplay, with the back section of the book reserved for "Activities" useful for drama students.

Philip Pullman's His Dark Materials Based on the Novels, adapted by Nicholas Wright. Nick Hern Books, 2003. This book has an introduction by Nicholas Wright, but not the one in the book of the same name published by Heinemann. Also, this edition lacks the "Activities" material found in that book. It is otherwise identical.

173

Prizes and Awards

1987

> Citation from *School Library Journal* for Best Books for Young Adults.
> Lancashire County Libraries/National and Provincial Children's Book Award.

1988

> *The Ruby in the Smoke* wins the Children's Book Award from the International Reading Association.
> Citation from the ALA (American Library Association) for Best Books for Young Adults.
> *The Ruby in the Smoke* wins the Preis der Leseratten from ZDF Television in Germany.

1989

> *Shadow in the Plate* is nominated for the Edgar Allan Poe Award from the Mystery Writers of America.

1995

> *Northern Lights* is shortlisted for the British Fantasy Award.

1996

> *Northern Lights* wins the Children's Book of the Year from British Book Awards.
> *Northern Lights* wins the Carnegie Medal from the British Library Association.
> *Northern Lights* jointly wins the Guardian Children's Fiction Prize.
> *The Firework-Maker's Daughter* (in the category of nine to eleven years) wins a Gold Award from the Nestlé Smarties Book Prize from Rowntree Mackintosh Co.
> *Clockwork* is shortlisted for the Carnegie Medal from the British Library Association.
> *The Golden Compass* (published in the United Kingdom as *Northern Lights*) wins the Book of the Year Award from the American Booksellers Association.

1997

Clockwork is shortlisted for the Carnegie Medal and the Whitbread Children's Book Award.

Clockwork wins the Smarties Silver Award.

The Subtle Knife wins Best Book of the Year from *Publishers Weekly.*

The Subtle Knife wins the Parents' Choice Gold Medal Book Award.

The Subtle Knife wins *Booklist* Editor's Choice.

2000

The Amber Spyglass wins the Children's Book of the Year from British Book Awards.

2001

Pullman wins the Author of the Year from British Book Awards.

The Amber Spyglass wins the Whitbread Children's Award.

The Amber Spyglass wins the Whitbread Book of the Year Award.

The Amber Spyglass is shortlisted for the World Fantasy Award for Best Novel.

His Dark Materials trilogy wins the May Hill Arbuthnot Honor Lecture Award.

2002

Pullman wins the Eleanor Farjeon Award.

Pullman wins Author of the Year Award from the American Booksellers Association.

2003

His Dark Materials is ranked third in BBC's public poll of Best Loved Novels.

His Dark Materials is shortlisted for the Audiobook of the Year from British Book Awards.

Pullman is shortlisted as the Author of the Year from British Book Awards.

Lyra's Oxford is shortlisted as the Children's Book of the Year from British Book Awards.

2004

The Tiger in the Well wins a Spoken Word Award in the category of Children's Fiction for the BBC Cover to Cover edition.

Pullman is named a Commander of the Order of the British Empire.

2005

Pullman is a joint winner for Sweden's Astrid Lindgren Memorial Award.

The Scarecrow and His Servant is shortlisted for the Carnegie Medal.

The Scarecrow and His Servant is shortlisted (in the category nine to eleven years) for the Nestlé Smarties Book Prize.

Appendices

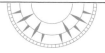

APPENDIX A

Fantasist Philip Pullman?

THERE ARE SOME THEMES, SOME SUBJECTS, TOO LARGE
FOR ADULT FICTION; THEY CAN ONLY BE DEALT WITH
ADEQUATELY IN A CHILDREN'S BOOK.
—Philip Pullman, "Far from Narnia,"
by Laura Miller *(The New Yorker)*

ust as Maine writer Stephen King will likely never escape his reputation (however undeserved) as a horror writer, I suspect Philip Pullman will not be able to convince most readers that he is neither a children's book author per se nor a fantasy writer. The former title he lives with, albeit with some discomfort, but the latter he vociferously repudiates, especially when critics, fans, and members of the media continue to insist that His Dark Materials is fantasy fiction.

Pullman has good reason to distance, and disassociate, himself from the fantasy genre. Though the genre has a long and distinguished history, the perception of the general public is that any book thus labeled means it's a work that has nothing to do with reality, which is where Pullman and fantasy books in general go their separate ways.

Although he admits that His Dark Materials clearly has elements of fantasy, he maintains—and successfully defends—his thesis that his book is one of "stark realism" and not what we traditionally imagine when we think of fantasy fiction.

In an online interview with www.powells.com, Pullman makes this fine and important distinction:

Dave: That raises one question right away. In an interview after the publication of *The Subtle Knife,* you denied that the trilogy was pure fantasy. You called it stark realism.

Pullman: I've had to deal with that frequently in the last couple days at this festival. People say, "What were you talking about? Of course you're writing fantasy!"

Well, when I made that comment, I was trying to distinguish between these books and the kind of books most general readers think of as fantasy: the sub-Tolkien thing involving witches and elves and wizards and dwarves. Really, those authors are rewriting *The Lord of the Rings.*

I'm trying to do something different: tell a story about what it means to grow up and become adult, the experience all of us have and all of us go through. I'm telling a story about a realistic subject, but I'm using the mechanism of fantasy. I think that's slightly unusual.

Pullman has a point—several, in fact. Since the publication of *The Lord of the Rings* in 1954, the shelves in the fantasy section groan under the weight of multi-part, epoch-sweeping sagas populated by stock characters.

Pullman, in a talk given at a Christian conference in the United Kingdom in 2002, explained that he was concerned His Dark Materials would be lumped in with the imitative Tolkien tomes and summarily dismissed as the book equivalent of cotton candy:

> Well, *that* was what I was embarrassed about: that I might be writing stuff that would turn out to be mere invention, superficial, arbitrary, trivial, with nothing to distinguish it externally from a thousand other big fat books crowding the fantasy shelves, all with titles like *The Doomsword Chronicles, Volume 17* or *Runequest* or *Orcslayer.* But I was anxious that there'd be nothing to distinguish my work from that sort of thing *internally,* either. I feared that I'd find myself assembling my characters in an arbitrary way from a kit of parts, and finding nothing important to say about them.

Of *The Lord of the Rings,* Pullman summarily dismisses it in his talk, saying that "The whole thing is an exercise in philological and social nostalgia, a work of immense triviality, candied like fruit in a Edwardian schoolboy's idea of fine writing."

The "stark reality" Pullman talks about, online and in interviews, refers to the weighty theme of *His Dark Materials,* which is pretty serious stuff:

> The theme of the [biblical] Fall, the fall away from grace and towards wisdom, the fall into embarrassment and self-consciousness: the theme of growing up. I saw how I could use all my various invented creatures—the dæmons, the armoured bears, the angels—to say something that I thought was true and important about us, about being human, about growing up and living and dying. My inventions were not real, but I hoped I could make them nonreal, and not unreal.

There's no question that Pullman succeeded—and brilliantly so. But the fact that *The Lord of the Rings* has stood the test of time for over a half century, sold millions of copies, and inspired countless critical texts and books examining its every aspect suggests that a legion of fans, readers, students, and academics see virtues in the book that have escaped Pullman's examination. After all, if *The Lord of the Rings* is, as Pullman says, a dismissible work, it asks the question: Why *hasn't* it been summarily dismissed by the world's readership? Even in his own country, when the BBC in 2003 polled the general public for its favorite book, *The Lord of the Rings* ranked number one, Pullman's own *His Dark Materials* ranked number three, *Harry Potter and the Goblet of Fire* ranked number five, and *The Lion, the Witch, and the Wardrobe* ranked number nine. (For the record, Pullman is also infamous for his attacks on Lewis's *The Chronicles of Narnia* as well, though he does enjoy Lewis's nonfiction.)

I agree that Pullman has written not only an entertaining but complex work, and that anchoring *His Dark Materials* to the Bible, *Paradise Lost,* and other classic texts gives his work a solid foundation on which he can construct his arguments about what he terms "the *truth* about the world, about life." But I disagree that all other fantasy, including *The Lord of the Rings,* is summarily dismissible. I think that a legion of today's fantasy writers, starting with Ursula K. Le Guin and Neil Gaiman (to name two of its most famous practitioners), would respectfully disagree.

As for WWJS (What would John [Ronald Reuel Tolkien] say), Tolkien speaks eloquently in a foreword to the second edition of *The Fellowship of the Ring:* "Some who have read the book, or at any rate have reviewed it, have found it boring, absurd, or contemptible; and I have no cause to complain, since I have similar opinions of their works, or of the kinds of writing that they evidently prefer."

It would be interesting to hear what Tolkien would say about His Dark Materials. I would like to think that even though he'd take issue with some of the content, Tolkien would also celebrate its many, varied virtues.

It would be just as interesting to hear what Pullman might have said to Tolkien, had he spoken to him on the evening he sat across from Tolkien at dinner at Oxford. Tolkien, as Pullman tells it, turned to the young student seated on one side of him and asked what he thought of *The Lord of the Rings*. The hapless student said he had never read it. Tolkien then turned to the student on the other side of him and asked about the curriculum. The lackluster response put a quick and merciful end to table conversation, and Tolkien quietly resumed his meal. Pullman merely observed the proceedings because he was not directly addressed.

⋙◆⋘

Labels aren't important, except to booksellers scratching their heads and wondering where to put Pullman's books on their shelves. For readers, who are far more interested in tales well told, the labels are likely meaningless, since a reader's priority is far more basic: Just tell me a story, the best way you know how; keep me entertained and teach me a little about our world. Bookselling is important to the retailers, but it's storytelling that's important to the reader. And in the end, it's the story-telling that really matters.

APPENDIX B

HELL TO PAY: PULLMAN'S SYMPATHY FOR THE DEVIL

MARK LAWSON: WHAT ABOUT THE FILM'S ANTIRELI-
GION THEME?
PHILIP PULLMAN: NOT ANTIRELIGION, BUT ANTIOP-
PRESSION, ANTIAUTHORITARIAN. IT'S OPPOSED TO THE
USE OF THEOCRACY FOR POLITICAL GAIN. THE CHURCH
IN LYRA'S WORLD IS VERY DIFFERENT FROM OUR OWN,
AS MANY THINGS ARE.
—from a talk at the Oxford Literary Festival in 2007

One of the biggest potential concerns that Pullman readers
have with the forthcoming film adaptation of *The Golden
Compass* is whether or not the studio is watering down the
film's more controversial elements to make it more palatable for the U.S.
audience of God-fearing, churchgoing conservatives who were instrumental in the box-office success of C. S. Lewis's *The Chronicles of
Narnia: The Lion, the Witch, and the Wardrobe* and director Mel Gibson's
The Passion of Christ.

If the book's attacks on organized religion are not toned down, what
might be the result? Perhaps due to fear of a backlash, it appears (based
on Pullman's recent comments at the Oxford Literary Festival) that New
Line Cinema has neatly solved the problem by positing that the attacks
in the book are not against the Church per se but against authority
figures who violate the public trust and abuse their power.

The fact remains, though, that His Dark Materials is unmistakably filled with religious references to priests, the Pope, and the Church that are clearly an attack on authority figures and focused on ecclesiastical matters, notably Roman Catholic.

As "Lord Asriel," the webmaster of hisdarkmaterials.org, explains: "Religion is without a doubt the most controversial point when it comes to adapting His Dark Materials. When Nicholas Wright adapted His Dark Materials for the stage, he retained all the religious elements, leading to various Christian organizations boycotting the show.

"Although Philip Pullman never meant to portray the Magisterium as a representation of our Church, almost all who have read the books have interpreted it that way. . . . For those of you that haven't read the books, the Magisterium is portrayed as a modern, totalitarian Inquisition."

But let's be honest: Pullman is of the devil's party, and he knows it. No question, when His Dark Materials was published, the *Catholic Herald* called it "the stuff of nightmares" and concluded it's "worthy of the bonfire." And speaking on behalf of Christian fundamentalists everywhere, Rupert Kaye, the chief executive of the Association of Christian Teachers, has gone on record calling the books "blasphemous." In fact, Kaye, who is up in arms against Pullman, writes that Pullman "actually set out with the much more modest intention of discrediting Christianity, undermining the Church, attacking God and giving C. S. Lewis a bloody nose!"

After his lackluster attempt at pummeling Pullman in print, Kaye concludes, "Personally, I wish that Philip Pullman had not written these books in this way; I wish they had not been marketed and sold as children's literature; I wish that they had not been an international best seller." In other words, Kaye disapproves of how Pullman wrote the books, disapproves of how his publishers marketed and sold the books (which, let's face it, Pullman had no control over), and disapproves of the fact that the books have sold so well. In short, it appears that Kaye would have preferred to see His Dark Materials remain relatively anonymous and hidden in bookstores or, better yet, not written at all. Pullman, you see, has not written satanic verses but satanic prose, according to Kaye, outraged almost beyond words. "Pullman is NOT attacking religion in general—he is attacking the Body of Christ. He is NOT critiquing all communities of faith—he is singling out Christians for assault."

It's fortunate for Pullman that he didn't live in the Middle Ages, when it was commonplace for the Church to execute people guilty of heresy (defined by the *Oxford English Dictionary* as "theological or religious opinion or doctrine maintained in opposition, or held to be contrary, to the Roman Catholic or Orthodox doctrine of the Christian Church, or, by extension, to that of any church, creed, or religious system, considered as orthodox").

All of this smacks of censorship and repression, and it's antithetical to a writer's duty, which is to speak the truth about the human condition from his or her unique perspective.

Pullman makes no bones about his religious views. On his website, he explains:

> I don't know whether there's a God or not. Nobody does, no matter what they say. I think it's perfectly possible to explain how the universe came about without bringing God into it, but I don't know everything, and there may well be a God somewhere, hiding away.
>
> Actually, if he is keeping out of sight, it's because he's ashamed of his followers and all the cruelty and ignorance they're responsible for promoting in his name. If I were him, I'd want nothing to do with them.

Whether Pullman is a heretic or a blasphemer is not the issue. The issue is whether Pullman—or any other writer, for that matter—has the right to write what he wishes, in his own way, without interference or censure, so the reading public can make up its own mind. Let the advocates of any organized religion put forth their strongest, most compelling arguments in matters of faith against Pullman's secular and humanistic views, and let the devil take the hindmost.

APPENDIX C

A Quick Guide to the Characters, Places, and Things Listed in Part 2

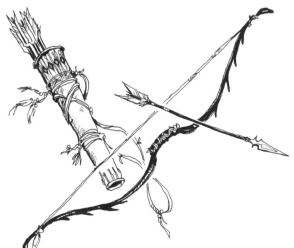

About the Contributors

George Beahm, who published his first book in 1975, on cartoonist Vaughn Bode, has worked in the book industry as a self-published author, regional publisher, author, book consultant, marketing director, book designer, and typesetter. In 2000, he founded Flights of Imagination, to promote the work of artists (notably Tim Kirk, Donato Giancola, and Britton McDaniel) by publishing prints, arranging art exhibits, and working on special projects. Using the "Meet Your Dæmon" feature on the official website for the *Golden Compass* movie, George is pleased to discover that his dæmon is an ocelot. George currently lives with his wife, Mary, in Williamsburg, Virginia. His websites include: georgebeahm.com and flightsofimagination.com.

———⇒◦⇐———

Tim Kirk is currently a design director for Kirk Design, which draws on his vast experience in conceptualization, content creation, and art direction at Walt Disney Imagineering, where he worked for twenty-two years. Among his many credits at Disney, Kirk was the overall senior designer for Tokyo DisneySea, a three-billion-dollar theme park. He also played a key role in conceptualizing the popular Disney MGM Studio Tour Park in the Walt Disney World Resort. A five-time Hugo Award winner for best art in the fantasy and science fiction field, Kirk's works have graced fanzines, calendars, limited edition books, and trade books for numerous publishers, including Ballantine, which issued his Tolkien illustrations, created as part of his master's degree in illustration, as the *1975 Tolkien Calendar*. A former artist for both Hallmark Cards and Current, Kirk has designed greeting cards, jigsaw puzzles, wrapping paper, stationery, and books. In June 2004, one of Kirk Design's projects made its debut: the Science Fiction Museum and Hall of Fame in Seattle, Washington. Kirk Design's website is www.kirkdesigninc.com. Using the

"Meet Your Dæmon" feature on the official website for the *Golden Compass* movie, Tim is pleased to discover that his dæmon is a wolf. Tim currently lives with his wife, Linda, in Long Beach, California.

———◆———

Philip Pullman—a former librarian, middle-school teacher, and lecturer—is the author of numerous children's books. The author of His Dark Materials and *Lyra's Oxford,* he is currently working on a sequel, *The Book of Dust.* He hazards a guess that his dæmon is a jackdaw or a magpie. He lives with his wife, Judith, near Oxford, England. His website is www.philip-pullman.com.

———◆———

Emma Raynaud: "I am thirty-five years old and live in Reading, Berkshire, with my husband and our three children. I discovered Lyra, my favorite of Philip Pullman's characters, after acquiring a U.S. first edition of *The Golden Compass* and have since become an avid reader and collector of his work. Living near Oxford, I was lucky enough to meet Philip Pullman recently at the Oxford Literary Festival 2007. It was during this trip that I took the photographs for this book."

———◆———

Nicola Priest was born in Cheshire in northwestern England. She spent many years living in Liverpool and one year in Paris. She now lives in Hampshire with her fiancé and helps him to run his landscape architecture practice. One of their current projects is a school playground inspired by Pullman's trilogy, His Dark Materials. Nicola's interests include films, reading, traveling, learning foreign languages, and supporting the Liverpool Football Club.

———◆———

Tiffany Vincent is an information technology analyst at a university. She lives in Cincinatti, Ohio, and spends her leisure time creating a collection of one-of-a-kind artifacts inspired by devices and curious things in fiction. Her website is at curiousgood.com. She lives with two cats and two dogs.

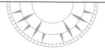

Tim Kirk's Painting
of Lyra in Oxford

Tim Kirk at home in Long Beach, California

"I wanted to emphasize Lyra's wildness. She's a feral child and the roofs of Oxford's colleges are her natural world and playground. I also wanted to emphasize her lonely situation: She is the possessor and interpreter of an alethiometer, with all the seriousness and cosmic portent that implies. She is supporting herself by draping her left arm over the gargoyle's neck (perched on a roof's edge, I'd want to hang onto something!), but I also wanted to subtly express Lyra's subconscious need for companionship and comfort. Heroine or not, she is still a twelve-year-old girl living in a world she only thought she understood."

The original pencil sketches: left, a discarded concept; right, the concept used

The rough painting for Tim Kirk's art depicting Lyra and Pantalaimon in Oxford

Tim Kirk's final artwork depicting Lyra and Pantalaimon in Oxford

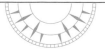

Acknowledgments

 our attention, please! Will the following people please stand up and take a bow. Don't be shy. You all deserve a round of applause.

To Tim Kirk, artist extraordinaire, whose artwork for this book (the color painting of Lyra and Pan in Oxford and numerous black-and-white illustrations) perfectly captures the essence of His Dark Materials. I am privileged to have him grace my books with his art, and grace my life with his friendship.

To Tania Seymour, my editor at Hampton Roads Publishing, whose unbridled enthusiasm for this book, tempered by her gimlet eye when it came to editing the manuscript, made the book measurably better.

To my friends at Hampton Roads Publishing, far too numerous to mention, but I'd like to specifically cite my friend and mentor, publisher Robert S. Friedman; CEO Jack Jennings, who is always open to a new, good book idea; Cindy Jennings, whose marketing and sales acumen ensures that this book will get out to all corners of the globe; and art director Jane Hagaman, who diligently worked to ensure that this book bore no resemblance to a book of academic text.

To Emma Raynaud who, while attending the Oxford Book Festival to hear Pullman's talk, went out of her way to take photos of Oxford especially for this book.

To Nicola Priest who, without the benefit of a tape recorder or secondary recordings, captured the roundtable discussion of Pullman, Forte, and Fink.

To Judith Evans at A. P. Watt who graciously allowed me to reprint Pullman's illuminating autobiographical piece, "I have a feeling all this belongs to me."

To Tiffany Vincent for photographs of two curious objects that she constructed.

To my wife, Mary, whose ideas about the content of this book helped shaped it for the better ("Make sure it's not too academic! Don't bore people! Don't give away too much of the story!"), and whose unremitting support in every other way has made the writing of this book a special joy.

And, finally, to Philip Pullman who wrote to me and clearly explained his position regarding books written about him and his work, which put me on the right path.

INDEX

Q

A photograph of Lyra and Will on the bench in Oxford garden, on the cube manufactured for the National Theatre

WE DON'T NEED A LIST OF RIGHTS AND WRONGS, TABLES OF DO'S AND DON'TS. WE NEED BOOKS, TIME, AND SILENCE. "THOU SHALT NOT" IS SOON FORGOTTEN, BUT "ONCE UPON A TIME" LASTS FOREVER.

—Philip Pullman

Hampton Roads Publishing Company

... for the evolving human spirit

HAMPTON ROADS PUBLISHING COMPANY
publishes books on a variety of subjects,
including metaphysics, spirituality,
health, visionary fiction, and other related topics.

For a copy of our latest trade catalog,
call toll-free, 800-766-8009,
or send your name and address to:

HAMPTON ROADS PUBLISHING COMPANY, INC.
1125 STONEY RIDGE ROAD • CHARLOTTESVILLE, VA 22902
E-mail: hrpc@hrpub.com • Internet: www.hrpub.com